Longbow Press Presents for Review:

Title: *Black Ice & Banana Peels*
Author: Mark Bender, Ph.D.   **Edition**: First
Number in Print: 2,500   **Pages**: 170
ISBN: 0-9722995-6-4   **LCCN**: 2002093748
Price: $12.95   **Pub. Date**: April, 2003

A copy of your review to the address below will be appreciated:

Longbow Press
PO Box 4221
Carlsbad CA 92018

760 434-7330   info@LongbowPress.com

BLACK ICE & BANANA PEELS

Getting A Grip On Your Mind

Mark Bender, Ph.D.

LONGBOW

PRESS

Longbow Press · Carlsbad, California

Black Ice & Banana Peels
Getting A Grip On Your Mind

Mark Bender

Published by:

Longbow Press
PO Box 4221
Carlsbad CA 92018

Orders: www.LongbowPress.com

e-mail: Contact@LongbowPress.com

ISBN 0-9722995-6-4

LCCN 2002093748

First Edition 2002

Contents

PART 2

THE SIBLINGS OF HEALING

PART 3

THE PARENTS OF LIFE PURPOSE

Acknowledgments

A number of teachers have been integral in my own healing process and, therefore, the development of this book. Foremost is Lansing Barrett Gresham, founder of Integrated Awareness® and Touchstone, a healing community in Cotati, CA. Lansing manifests a truly awesome ability to lovingly and safely support the discovery, for oneself, of the healing power within. For those inspired to inquire further, I cannot recommend him too highly. Other teachers that have been influential and inspirational include Hugh Milne of Big Sur, CA, Harriet Goslins of Laguna Beach, CA, Daniel Bianchetta of Big Sur, CA and Robert Raleigh of Las Cruces, NM.

A variety of authors have also contributed to my understanding of the healing process. Notable among these are Idries Shah, Franklin Jones (also known as Da Free John, Da Avahbasa, etc.) and Moshe Feldenkrais.

Thanks to the friends that gave me feedback on the manuscript: Samantha Nieman, Danny Shearer, Ruth Sheldon, Doreen Quinn and Carole Valetta. Thanks also to the following for their contributions: R. W. Davignon – editing, Tamara Spurr and Michael Spackman – cover art, Andrew Mansker – desktop publishing, Frank Benages and Bill Floyd of Fidlar Doubleday – printing.

Note to the Reader

New discoveries and technologies are changing our daily lives at an accelerating rate, yet our ability to manage our affairs and to get along with friends, family, neighbors and other nations frequently seems inadequate and the tasks overwhelming. I wrote this book to address the fundamental challenge involved in relating to ourselves, others and God; how we use our mind. Without, at least, some understanding of the ways in which our mind functions, we are at the mercy of this master controller.

The information contained in this book is not a cure-all nor is it intended to be a replacement for anyone who may be assisting you in your healing process. It is, rather, an aid on your path of self-discovery. There are a variety of important aspects of the healing process which are discussed only peripherally here, in order to focus on this particular topic.

The purpose of this book is to educate. The author and the publishing company shall have neither liability nor legal responsibility to any person or entity with respect to any loss or damage caused, or alleged to have been caused, directly or indirectly by the information contained in the book.

If you do not wish to be bound by the above, you may return the book for a full refund.

This book is dedicated to

Siena

for her love, support, humor and
her relentless desire to evolve.

Introduction

Our mind's power to control and hide, at the same time, is truly awesome. There may be no need to look further than this for proof of the existence of God. More about that later. Our mind's goal is survival and it will aggressively pursue this agenda at the expense of the rest of our capacities. Its basic means of survival is control. In order to control effectively, it must initially convince us that it is doing something critical to our well-being. To continue to control, as we develop the ability to recognize our mind at work, it must learn to operate behind the scenes.

In order to hide, our mind gets us to believe that there is no distinction between it and the rest of who we are. Our mind makes itself synonymous with the whole of our existence. Of course, there's much more to you than your mind, but how often do you remember that, especially under stress? Whenever you're judging something as right or wrong, strategizing your way out of discomfort, figuring out what something means; at that moment you are your mind and you have lost contact with the other parts of you, which would otherwise be available to help.

This book brings to light how our mind works; the different ways our mind overtly and covertly both gets in our way and, at the same time, through language, energy and behavior, shows us how to move in a healthier direction. It may sound, as you read this, like your mind is an enemy that must be rooted out and eliminated. Not at all. The wonder of our mind is that while it continually leads us to stumble and sometimes fall, it is, at the same time, showing us exactly what to do in order to heal, grow and evolve.

When I talk about our mind, I'm referring to that part of us that started out as our protector, ran amok with that agenda and continues to carry out its self-assigned role, even when no longer needed. There is another aspect of us called The Mind. It is creative, vast and expansive—a part of the Universal Mind. Though our minds are fearful, The Mind knows no fear. Our minds label, categorize, compare and are obsessed with right and wrong. The Mind laughs at those distinctions. While our minds seek control, The Mind exists as consciousness and evolution.

Everything presented in this book is a model. It is a way of exploring questions that are intimately connected with the experience of humanity. Each of us has formed his/her own model and belief system of the way things work. If the material presented here doesn't help you in some way, throw it out. I only ask that you explore it before you discard it. Don't toss it away because it doesn't immediately agree with your world-view. And don't keep it if your experience leads you elsewhere.

The book is divided into three parts. Part 1 is about fear and doubt—how our minds use a variety of mechanisms to create an illusion of safety and the misperception that we know what we're doing. Part 2 is about healing and learning—the process by which we come to recognize what our minds are actually doing and how we can use that awareness to move in the direction of healthier choices. Part 3 focuses on life purpose—the relationship of self-trust and consciousness.

One of the challenges in reading a book about your mind, especially about how your mind attempts to control, is that your mind *is* the habitual way you use to take in information. When this information threatens the status quo, your mind finds a way to discount, misperceive or simply ignore the data. To counteract this, I suggest that you take your time in reading, focus on feeling what is being said, rather than thinking about it, and reread as much as is necessary to embody the information. To assist you, quotes, stories and slogans have intentionally been left out so that you will be challenged to feel for yourself what is being conveyed.

PART 1

THE CHILDREN OF
FEAR & DOUBT

1

CONTROL

How to run the show while pretending you're not

When we are born, we are entirely dependent on outside help for survival. Our nervous system is designed with a few reflexes to get us started, such as sucking, the ability to give simple signals to the environment, such as making sounds of discomfort or pleasure, the senses to take in and process information, and a predisposition for learning. We would not survive without others to feed, clean and provide shelter for us.

As infants, our minds have only a very rudimentary existence, initially occupied with little more than pleasure or pain. Our brains receive volumes of information while our minds focus on interpreting the information in a meaningful and useful way. Food, touch, light, sound, warmth and varied stimuli are usually perceived as pleasurable and supporting survival. Their absence is perceived as painful and a threat to survival. These are accurate perceptions. Without some of these things, we would not survive and without the rest we would not thrive.

As toddlers we are not able to distinguish between survival needs and other needs. We generalize and lump things together so that being startled by a loud noise or not having a desired toy at hand is perceived as the same kind of threat to survival as not being fed. Children cry easily and often because of this threat generalization and their limited variety of responses to the environment. We have experiences, at a very young age, which lead us to generalize about the way the environment responds to us. Our minds start to believe survival is threatened, even when it is not. As we grow, we generalize our survival needs even further so that the expressed love and approval of our family members and caregivers become as important to our survival as shelter and food.

We also learn that our ability to influence the environment, including the people in it, is limited. We learn that the big people are in control of most of the things we want and would choose to provide ourselves, if we could. We come to believe that getting our needs met is dependent on pleasing the big people. Again, this is largely an accurate perception. If the people we depend upon do not provide what is needed, we have very limited ability to provide it for ourselves. Our ability to control the environment and others becomes equivalent with survival. Loss of control is perceived as a threat to survival.

Our attempts to gain control, so as to minimize survival threats, become, in effect, the identification and solution of various problems. When we can't control others directly, it makes sense to learn to control them indirectly. When we can't control others at all, it makes sense to control ourselves. We believe we can accomplish this control by identifying the problem and then developing a solution. If, for example, my perception is that mom doesn't love me, I have to find a way to please her so that she will love me, or at least take care of me—otherwise my survival is at risk.

Soon, solving the apparent problem becomes equated with regaining control and reducing the survival threat that is presented. If the problem remains unsolved for a significant length of time, anxiety increases. When the problem is solved, anxiety decreases. Our mind, in order to maintain control, convinces us that the problem it's trying to fix is outside of our mind—in the environment, other people or in some other part of us—*not in our mind itself.* This is key to understanding how our mind hides what it's doing.

In this way, life becomes a series of problems to be solved or fixed, keeping us very busy riding the roller coaster of success and failure. We develop a personality, the outward manifestation of our mind, which becomes our stand-in for open, honest and congruent interactions with the environment and others. We need this front, we believe, because our mind is continually telling us that maintaining control is what keeps us alive and that being genuine is too risky. In order to control ourselves, we often resort to coercion. We force ourselves to do things that, if we did not believe our survival was at stake, we would not even consider. In doing this, we override our feelings, our wishes, our dreams. We frequently go against our true desires, seeking instead to be liked, acknowledged, approved or to grab whatever small token is coming our way.

What is it that we're all so busy trying to control? Relationships? Other people? The future? Ourselves? That is the outward appearance of things. What we are trying to control is fear. Our mind tells us that if we can control people, things and situations, we will be okay. Attempting to control our fear around relationships becomes the driving force behind much of what we do. We are afraid of being alone, afraid of being unloved, afraid of being rejected, afraid of feeling, afraid of not feeling, afraid of being old, poor, diseased, ugly, disappointed, frustrated, hurt, dead; it's a virtually endless list. The funny thing is that all of our control does nothing to lessen the fear. Indeed, all the effort we put into controlling our fear only convinces us that our fears are justified! And all that struggle and strain does virtually nothing to prevent us from feeling all those things we want to hide from. Fear is what we want to avoid, and our minds create a world where that fear is continuous. This is another key to how our minds operate; continually, though unintentionally, creating the very thing we're trying to avoid, thereby further reinforcing the apparent need for even greater control.

What's the alternative? Well, since you're going to experience these feelings and thoughts anyway, maybe it's part of the plan, the journey, the human experience. Maybe a first step lies in remembering that you've already felt the fear and all the other stuff you're afraid of and you didn't die. Life went on. Yes, some people do get so overwhelmed by these feelings and thoughts that they choose not to go on, but you're reading this, so you're still here.

It's also helpful to understand that what began as fear has become anxiety. Fear is what our bodies feel when, for example, a car almost hits us. It's a physiological reaction to a situation, happening now, that threatens our physical survival. Anxiety, however, is our mind's reaction to the future it has imagined. Your mind looks into the future, sees an undesirable outcome based on past experience and then reacts to the non-existent event. Our mind relies on the past as its predictor for the future because that's the source, it believes, for our emotional pain. In this way, our mind finds further justification for its fear and doubt.

Our minds are brilliant. They identify a genuine need (survival), expand that need so that it appears to exist even when it doesn't (generalization), attach a strong unpleasant emotion to that need (anxiety), create an indispensable role for themselves in meeting that need (problem identification and solution), and convince us that the problem is outside of our mind (job security)!

What's truly odd about this is that, when it comes to our growth and healing, there are no problems to be solved. Our mind labels something as a problem and, due to its power over our perceptions, we accept this label without question. What our mind labels as a problem becomes something that we believe we must fix in order to survive. Once we identify a problem, we will automatically devote great energy and time to finding a solution, and thus our mind's control is again reinforced.

We start to lose ourselves in order to fix the identified problem. "I have to make more money, find my soul mate, change my looks, get a better job, be more sensitive, become a better lover, not get so anxious, make everyone happy," and a hundred other demands. We stay very busy coercing ourselves to fix those things that we think we should be able to influence—our appearance, relationships, living situation, finances and the like—

all to maintain the illusion of control. We seek out experts who offer the right medication, vacation, therapy or transformative experience. We change our hair, our style of dress, our living situation, our speech, our diet. It doesn't matter. Our mind will find a way to control everything we do because it's still running the show. It does this by filtering our perceptions so that almost nothing gets through other than what fits into our mind's existing program; a program that says the problem is outside our mind when, actually, it is our mind itself which keeps the merry-go-round turning by labeling everything as an external problem to be solved. It's like a faulty software program that keeps telling you the problem is in the hardware, because it can't recognize it's own errors.

If you've been paying some attention to your life, you may have gotten the idea, by now, that control doesn't work very well. Look at the process of trying to change others. When we don't ask for or say what we want directly, we find covert ways of expressing ourselves. We may think we're fooling the other person, but he/she feels, at that moment or later, that there is a subtext to our message, which, while not being communicated through words, is still there. If I'm saying one thing and intending another, you will understandably be on guard or angry when you figure out my true intentions.

Control, in the form of trying to fix yourself, similarly does not work very well. After all, if you were going to make a quick radical transformation, why hasn't it already happened? How long have you been trying to fix the same things about yourself? Years? Your whole life? It may seem odd, but trying to fix yourself is no more effective than trying to change others. You are not, after all, a car with a broken fan belt. The many other parts of you, like your mind, also resent being viewed as broken. Additionally, you can't use your mind to change your mind. That's like trying to repair a flat tire while still driving the car or trying to squeeze five quarts of water in a one-gallon bottle. Real change requires a different position and perspective and a bigger container to provide the space for using more of yourself.

* * *

Q: *How do I take in new information, which may threaten my mind, without using my mind?*

A: There are a number of methods to circumvent our habitual style of filtering, censoring and misperceiving what is around us. Gratitude is one way. How often do we acknowledge and appreciate the parts of ourselves, like our minds, that have allowed us to survive, grow and develop? Do we thank our skeleton, muscles, nerves and organs, which are also programmed for survival and are continually working for our well-being? How is our mind to know that its original job of ensuring our survival is complete if we do not, in some way acknowledge it?

Not only is gratitude important as a marker of a job well done, but it also serves as a way to respond when your mind is active. In other words, when I catch my mind trying to control something and I remember that it's just doing what it's programmed for, I thank it for its input and now, since I have recognized my mind at work, I can let it go and respond differently. It's like a catch and release program for your mind.

Another way is to recognize that we have many opportunities to learn what we need. Because our mind starts its self-assigned program of control for survival purposes, new information, which could undermine its role, is often perceived as a threat to successfully carrying out its mission. New information is rarely new. We are continually being exposed to an abundance of information coming from our bodies, other people and the environment, which, if we can let it in, shows us a way to heal. We often think that we are hearing, seeing or feeling something for the first time because our minds are so successful at misperceiving information and at maintaining their role as the supervisor who gets to choose what gets in, what gets altered and what gets ignored.

In hindsight, this may seem sad because we've had so many exposures to information which, if we had taken it in and used it, would have allowed us to heal much sooner. The good news is that we are continually being exposed to everything we need to evolve, and if we don't get it the first time, which we almost never do because of our mind's control, we may get it the 10th or the 100th time. Since control implies being all-knowing, our mind will usually decide we must be either stupid or slow because of all those missed chances. However, we can also use this apparently universal requirement for repetition to lighten up on ourselves, since this plane of existence is structured so that we have multiple opportunities to learn everything we need. If you were flying a plane on autopilot and for some reason you temporarily passed out, you would probably be thankful, when you woke up, that the autopilot was working. Your mind is not an enemy. It's like an autopilot that's stuck in the on position. And it will stay that way until we find out how to turn it off.

Another key to taking in new information is to listen. When our bodies, the environment or other people speak to us about anything related to change, learning or healing, our mind, being keenly attuned to filtering out anything that threatens its position, will get more active than usual. If it didn't, you might hear what was actually being said. When you notice that you're thinking, planning your response, fidgeting, not paying attention or one of the many other ways to not listen, this is again a clue that your mind is trying to control what's going on.

We get all kinds of messages, at home and at school, about what good boys and girls do. Good boys and girls are quick, smart, responsive, etc. Your mind takes these in as things it needs to do, all the time, to be loved and survive. It's as if, when someone is speaking to you, you're going to be graded on how smart and quick you can show you are in response to them, which usually involves either agreeing with them or explaining to them how they are mistaken. What would happen if you listened, instead, is that you would take in what was said and feel it. You would feel who that person is through their words, voice tone, body language, energy field, etc. You would feel who you are in relation to all of that. You would take as much time as needed and then respond in a way that reflected how that information impacted you. Yes, there probably will be some period of silence during this process. If the other person is uncomfortable with your silence you can say howdy to their mind at work! Listening is giving yourself permission to be changed by what you hear.

There are some people who listen very well and don't particularly hear the words being said. They focus, instead, on feeling the words and letting them enter their body by means other than filtering them through their mind. In this way they are able to take in information, which is valuable for their learning and healing, without activating their mind's protective armor. If you find, when you listen to someone, that you get caught up in the words, get confused or are missing something, experiment with feeling what they're saying. Feel it in your heart, your bones, your gut or wherever works for you. You could even ask them to repeat it without making that mean anything about you. In this way, you may be able to feel what is being said in a way that makes more sense and has more integrity than if you focused on the words. Most people, most of the time, are speaking from their minds, from a place of control. Not focusing on the words allows you to also hear what is not being said, which is often more valuable and shows much about their mind at work. In this way our minds' hiding becomes visible.

Being in The Mind, feeling connected rather than separated, is a further way, perhaps the essential way, in which we can take in new information. It's challenging, at first, to do this directly because being in The Mind requires not being in your mind. Each time you step out of your mind by recognizing it at work or through other experiences, you are, for a moment, in The Mind. People feel The Mind differently at different times: acceptance, self-trust, ease, spirit, laughter. As you spend less time in your mind, you will automatically spend more time in The Mind.

Recognizing your mind at work, feeling gratitude, listening and acknowledging that we have never-ending opportunities to learn are just a few ways to help ourselves take in information that may be valuable for our healing and learning. We begin to see that the very ways that our mind uses to keep us trapped in the maze are, at the same time, showing us the way out.

Q: *What do you mean when you say there are no problems to be solved?*

A: Problems are whatever our mind says they are. Is it a problem that you haven't found the perfect relationship, don't make enough money, can't seem to have a pleasant conversation with your teenage son or daughter? You may not like these things, but does that mean they are problems for which you must find solutions? What we habitually do with problems is make them mean something about us. Do we make them mean something good about ourselves? No, we don't. We make everything that our mind has identified as a problem mean that we or the other person are somehow deficient, inadequate, not good enough. It's as if having a problem comes to mean that we have an incurable disease. Our mind says it must mean that because otherwise we wouldn't have that problem!

What if our mind is simply stuck on its own labels? What if these problems don't mean that there's something wrong with us? What if these problems aren't problems at all? What if they're simply things we would like to be different. I'd like to sleep better. I want us to stop killing each other. I'd prefer my father not have Parkinson's disease, etc. Are these problems that I need to fix in order to feel good about myself? No, they're things I'd like to change and am working on. That I haven't found solutions for them is not a reflection of who I am as a human being.

Every time we identify a problem that we believe must be solved in order for us to feel better about ourselves, our mind has again succeeded at exercising control over our perceptions and actions. When we identify something as a problem, whether it's about us or others, we have, in effect, labeled ourselves as the problem. You would think that identifying something as a problem would marshal our best ability to find a solution. Yet, when it comes to the problems our mind identifies about relationships and who we are, the very act of calling it a problem, causes us to limit the resources we can bring to bear because we're already feeling wrong or bad about even having the problem. There are no problems to be solved because there are no problems to begin with—only those things that our mind has labeled as problems in order to help guarantee that it will continually be able to maintain control, by identifying what it thinks needs to be fixed.

2

JUDGMENT

Comparing my rights with your wrongs

Have you ever noticed how much you and others want to be right? Politics, money, love, fitness, weather, laws, happiness, the fastest or shortest or least expensive way to do something; it doesn't even matter what you're talking about. What matters is being right. Why? Will you die if you're not right? Will you stop being loved if you're not right? Will you fall off the planet if you're not right? Well, yes. That's what your mind tells you.

Feel that momentary high that comes with being right or, at least, the other person being wrong. Feel that temporary relief of anxiety that happens when someone tells you your action or opinion is the right one. If you're not able to recall these feelings about being right, recall how you felt the last time you were wrong about something. It's the flip side of the same coin. It's the coin that parents, teachers, peers and, starting in childhood, our mind, throw us all the time, and we're stuck with whichever side lands facing up. This time you're right, next time you're wrong. It's not much different than a game of chance and we stake our entire well being on it every moment.

If you compared emotions to drugs, the complex of emotions that surrounds the high of being right is, perhaps, the most addictive drug your mind can experience. We're afraid of being wrong because our minds equate that with being abandoned, unloved, unaccepted, a failure, etc. Being right becomes the same as being good, accepted, lovable.

How did this come about? How did we get caught in this never-ending game of chance without ever having decided to play? We're taught, from a very early age, that learning the difference between right and wrong is essential to becoming happy, healthy and well-adjusted boys and girls. Parents, other family members, and later, teachers and peers seem to have a keenly developed sense of right and wrong which they believe is their duty to pass along to us. The same words—right and wrong—are used to help us learn a whole variety of different things, as if they applied equally well to all of them: data, ideas, beliefs, thoughts, feelings, behaviors, etc. It's as though these two magic words can somehow encompass the whole of what it means to be human and show us the way to true happiness.

Where did we get our version of right and wrong? Is it genetic? Was it encoded in our brains at birth? Or did its meaning and application come from the same people who worked so hard to teach us its value? And where did those experts get it from? We use these two words and pass them along to the next generation as if everyone was in full agreement about their usage. However, what's right in our culture may be wrong in someone else's. What's right in this moment may be wrong in the next. What's right from where I'm standing may be wrong from your perspective. Even what has been long accepted as a scientific certainty has often later been proven incorrect and thrown out.

If right and wrong were so clear and self-evident, how come we spend so much time arguing over them? We disagree with each other as individuals, groups, communities and nations. We become wedded to our version of right and wrong as if it were gospel and we follow it blindly, unaware of where it leads. Think of all the grief, pain and death that have resulted from the way we use laws, judicial systems, police, national defense, etc., all based on someone's belief that their rights have been wronged. Think of all the indigenous peoples, animals and resources harmed by individuals, businesses, religions or nations exercising their rights. Thus far, our addiction to right and wrong and our dependence on their use as a justification for our behavior don't seem to have done much for our ability to get along with each other.

Struggle, dilemma, confusion, etc., usually stem from wanting to be right and failing to do so. If using right and wrong, in this way, does little, if anything, to further our growth and learning, how is it that we are so stuck on the need to reduce everything to right and wrong? Well, our mind tells us to, and you know it's always right, except when it's wrong. Our mind has to know, has to distinguish, has to determine to a certainty, what is right and wrong because without that, it could not control everything so rigidly. It could not tell us what to do, how to behave, how to change others and ourselves and how to worry about all the important stuff.

All this activity that your mind is engaged in is based, originally, on the need for survival and, later, on perceived threats to survival. Your mind just never noticed that you grew up and that your survival is actually no longer dependent on pleasing others, being a good boy or girl or being right. Our language reflects how much power our mind still exerts over this. Children can often be heard arguing about it. "I'm right!" and "You're wrong!" get repeated so often that, sometimes, they don't even remember what they were talking about. As we grow older we develop other forms of this including "That's ridiculous!" "You don't know what you're talking about!" and more colorful versions of the same message. They all boil down to "You're wrong!" When this happens, the conversation is no longer about the relative merits of our positions, no longer about preferences or what you like or believe. It's solely about who will come out on top. "Being right" is elevated, in that moment, to a higher plane of existence. It's as if, when you're right, the entirety of who you are is correct, justified, lovable, pure, whole and superior. And when you're wrong, well, forget about it; you just never want to be wrong. And, even when you do come out on top, the high is momentary, the victory feels hollow. Sure, your mind scored a point but now it's already looking for the next thing to control.

What if being right and being wrong are virtually the same thing, the top and bottom of the same treadmill? Win an argument with a co-worker or your spouse and you're up. Someone cuts you off in traffic or you forget a friend's birthday and you're down. When you start running on a treadmill, what started out as the top and bottom quickly become indistinguishable. They merge into one continuous track but you know you've got to stay on top and keep moving; otherwise, you'll fall off. How's this treadmill been working for you so far? Are those right and wrong muscles firm and strong or do you need to keep exercising them? If you decided to get off, how would you do it?

I like mint chip ice cream and you like chocolate ripple; not much there to pull us into a debate of right and wrong. But what if I tell you that the Yankees, my team, are better than the Orioles, your team. Now, by making a comparison, I'm inviting you to tell me why that isn't so. I'll probably respond that, of course, you don't know what you're talking about and we're off and running. As in this case, it may be in jest or not very serious but what about a similar situation where each side has a weapon? What if each side has an army and they're talking about national boundaries or water rights?

Even when we don't use the words, right and wrong, that's what were arguing about because each side is making a comparison, which labels one set of actions, values or beliefs as better than another. Our minds love comparisons because they use them to determine the best or most right way of doing something. In order to control, our minds must have that information. Comparisons allow our minds to quickly label something as good or bad, right or wrong. It's our mind's need to make an immediate jump into certainty that hooks us into going round and round about so many things, which are simply a matter of preference.

Maybe you have certain religious beliefs that I don't share. Or maybe in your culture, women are treated differently than in mine. Maybe we disagree about love or God or the use of corporal punishment or the death penalty or euthanasia or drug legalization or abortion or national defense or globalization or terrorism. Who's right and who's wrong? There are virtually an infinite number of preferences and beliefs we may not share. The point is that all these things we have opinions about simply are. There is no inherent right or wrong in them. If mint chip ice cream is mint chip ice cream, not right or wrong, then the death penalty is the death penalty, also not right or wrong. Letting something be neither right nor wrong does not necessarily imply that you agree with it or don't have an opinion or are unwilling to express how you feel. What it does is allow others to have their preferences as well. And, when we don't feel the need to defend ourselves, we can actually listen to what is being said.

We make judgments, which are value labels of right or wrong, about things and about each other and these judgments take the place of genuine communication. When I say, "You're wrong," I'm making the whole of who you are equivalent to your opinion about a particular thing. But aren't you much more than just your opinion? Aren't you more than your mind? And isn't it possible that your opinion or preference or belief may change over time?

When you're running on the right/wrong treadmill, it's like your mind is shouting in your ear (it doesn't mean to; it wants to stay out of sight), "Hey, look at me! Guess who's in charge now!" If we hear this shout, we begin to recognize that our mind is running the show and this brings up the possibility of making another choice. If I were to verbalize that process, my inner dialogue might sound something like this. "Wait a doggone second here. My mind started steering the boat when I wasn't looking and now I'm headed for the rocks! I'm going to take the wheel again." When my mind isn't in charge, I can see that neither of us are right or wrong for our particular beliefs or preferences.

When we express our beliefs, preferences and opinions, as such, the words right and wrong no longer seem to serve much purpose and we can then see that our behaviors simply are what they are. Not liking something doesn't mean it's wrong; it means you don't like it. You can work to change it, you can accept it, you can study it; there's lots of options when you don't close the door by making it wrong. We're so stuck on being right because our minds equate being right with survival and being wrong with abandonment and death. We're so stuck on making the other person wrong because our mind can then believe we're right. Making judgments becomes a habit that grew out of our mind's survival misperceptions. How actually, can you or anyone else be right or wrong about opinions or preferences? You can't. Imagine making a mistake and not making yourself wrong for it. Maybe even laughing about it. Changing that habit is dependent on recognizing your mind at work.

How many times a day do we make judgments about ourselves or others? 10? 50? 100? It becomes so habitual that we don't even know it's happening. The way we and others talk, walk, act, look, think, feel, behave, believe; there's a never-ending supply of material about which we can make the most damning judgments—serious mind candy. It occurs because our mind must continually, for our very survival, it believes, hold on to being right. We're incessantly seeking validation of who we are in the hope that we will be loved. Do we get to make all these judgments for free? Hardly. There's a high cost associated with judgment. Every time you make a judgment about yourself or others, you contract, you get smaller. To hold a judgment you have to contract those muscles where that judgment resides: your jaw, throat, stomach, neck, back, shoulders, etc. Or did you think that being self-righteous was an expansive feeling that magically connects you with the universe? These contractions not only continuously consume energy but they interefere with your freedom of movement, freedom of choice and, over time, actually change your physical structure.

Our minds have to continually simplify everything, make it black and white. Our minds learned this from our bodies. Our brain constantly makes adjustments in the levels of hormones, neurotransmitters, etc. to keep everything in balance. It does this by continually measuring the levels of these molecules in our body and determining if there's too much or too little. Our minds borrowed this form of monitoring and use it for things to which it doesn't apply. Can you really be too thoughtful, too patient, too opinionated, not happy enough, not tall enough, not beautiful enough? According to whom? In what situation?

Your mind uses right and wrong as a shorthand form of communication. The simpler and easier it is to categorize, for your mind, the more it can maintain control. Right and wrong are about as simple and black and white as you can get. Well, not exactly. Our minds need to see things as opposites, even when they're not. Positive and negative; they're opposites, right? Actually, they're the two ends of the same scale that measures value or electrical charge. Light and dark? The two ends of the spectrum of visible light. Large and small? Right and wrong? Good and bad?

All of these are values which our mind will try to keep as opposites in order to hold onto certainty. Actually, one would not exist without the other. Further, it's quite difficult to tell where one changes into the other. At what point does light become dark, or warm become cool? Our mind is often vague about these distinctions, especially in the middle of the spectrum. So, what our mind takes as apparently self-evident and clearly defined categories, are not that black and white, after all.

Sometimes we pretend we're not judging. We call this "withholding judgment." This is like saying, "I'm not going to judge you or this thing right now but I reserve my right, at any later time, to make my judgment." It works about as well as withholding breathing. How do we know when judgment is running amok? Quite simple. Any time our mind labels something as either right or wrong, we're judging. So then, what about judgment itself? Isn't judgment wrong? There's our mind again! That's the tricky part. Judgment, like air, bubblegum, trees and the belief in right and wrong, simply is.

Knowing is another way that our mind holds onto right and wrong. When I know how to do something, which implies the best way, whether it's taking the seed out of an avocado, getting to the airport in the least amount of time, communicating effectively or making love, my mind is easily threatened by the possibility that there might be missing information. It's threatening because, in order to believe that I'm in control, I have to already know whatever's important to the matter at hand, and the idea that I might not know something relevant threatens that control.

Knowing, then, actually gets in the way of learning. Not knowing, so that you are open to a new experience, facilitates and promotes learning. This is not the same as pretending ignorance. That's just pretending. Not knowing is putting aside your prior knowledge, experience, beliefs, judgments, etc., while you participate in the present experience. This is sometimes referred to as beginner's mind. We do not do this easily. Good boys and girls, after all, know the answer before the question is asked. Good boys and girls have to appear that they know even when they don't.

There is much we don't know. We can make good guesses but we don't know what others feel or believe about something until we hear it from them. We frequently don't even know how we feel about things until we're actually faced with that question or situation. So another benefit of not knowing is that you get to say three little words that are frequently considered not okay in educated society; "I don't know." You can say them without being wrong for not knowing. Of course, another way you'll be able to tell your mind is hard at work is if it comes out as, "I don't know" (because I'm stupid, slow, etc.)

The most disabling way we judge is when we judge ourselves. It's a lot more frequent than our judgment of others simply because we're always around ourselves. The cost of this is lack of self-trust, not liking yourself, anxiety, depression, guardedness and, frequently, poor health. Why so much self-judgment? Our mind values control as the highest good, and if we can't control others, the only option left is to try and control ourselves. We'll even take on the role of being bad, wrong, stupid, a failure, etc., as a way of maintaining control. The hope is that we can get others to agree with us that, at least, we're right in our self-perception of being wrong. It's our mind's way of intentionally being wrong in order to be right. And, making ourselves wrong gives us the false hope that we can somehow, one day, pray to God, please, please, please, finally be right. What a mind!

* * *

Q: *How can I teach my children to succeed in the world without teaching them right and wrong?*

A: Some people will say, "You have to teach kids right from wrong!" When people say that, you may hear several things. They want their children to be happy and to succeed. Right and wrong is the way they were taught and they turned out okay. They don't know any other way. And they're concerned about raising their kids in the right way (there it is again!)

Of course, we want our children to be happy and succeed and we actually have no control over that, though our minds will insist otherwise. The thing to do, then, is to model, in your own behavior, what you'd like for them, practice the desirable behaviors with them and let them know when they do something that is dangerous or undesirable. All of that can be done without the use of right and wrong.

When we employ right and wrong with children we are, unintentionally, telling them that these are absolutes which everyone adheres to. In other words, we are training them not to think or feel or pay attention to what's going on inside and around them and that, instead, they need to behave according to these supposedly universal external rules and values. What we think we're teaching children when we focus on right and wrong is a set of values. What the child is actually learning is that some people, depending on their size, status or force of will, get to dictate thought and behavior to others. The child, now feeling in a one-down position, begins to seek out situations where he/she can dictate to others. The values get lost in the desire to move into a one-up position. And this becomes the pattern of a lifetime.

Whenever our mind judges us to be less than someone else, it creates some opportunity to make up for it. By the time we're no longer children, it's become very difficult to get out of this habitual and painful cycle. Children, out of their need to please adults, turn right and wrong behaviors into right and wrong feelings, thoughts and lives.

Teaching right and wrong isn't even the most effective way to communicate desirable behaviors to children. What they want, more than anything, is to be loved and to avoid feeling unloved. Imagine this; a child is visiting a neighbor's house and picks up a glass vase to look at it. It slips out of his hand and breaks on the floor. At that moment his mother walks in, sees what has happened, grabs his wrist and yells that he's wrong and bad, that she told him not to touch anything and that he'll be punished when he gets home. You can imagine how the child feels or how you would feel in the same situation. Now imagine the same event and this time, when his mother finds him, she initially doesn't do anything. Instead, she's being with herself for a moment to register her own feelings and then making a choice as to what she wants to do. This, in of itself, gets the child's attention in a new way. Then she quietly takes him aside and, with direct eye contact, tells him how she feels: disappointed, angry, sad, frustrated, whatever is true for her at that moment, and she says nothing that labels him or his behavior as bad or wrong.

Telling other people, especially children, how we feel, carries much more impact than telling them our judgments. In the first scenario, the child doesn't know much, for sure, except, maybe, that he broke some kind of rule. He can make some guesses about how mom feels but he doesn't really know because she hasn't told him. In the second scenario, he knows exactly how she feels and since, as a child, he's especially attentive to her feelings, he is likely to be a lot more impacted by her communication.

It's a commonly held belief that children need to be disciplined immediately after the event. Sometimes, immediately works, though you lose a valuable chance to think and feel about it. Often a delay of several hours or even a day has more impact because the child has a reason (the unexpected delay) and the time to think about what happened. And when mom gives herself some time to not only feel what is true for her but to also plan how she wants to respond, she sets an excellent example for her son. There are lots of options available other than the quick labeling of behavior as right or wrong. Maybe she senses that he's already afraid, just because he broke the vase and she hugs him in response to his fear. She could choose to say nothing until after she gets home. She could get a broom and sweep it up or give him the broom. She could have him do a written or verbal apology, etc.

The people who are telling us we're right or wrong are just as trapped on the right/wrong treadmill as we are. If we help our children not to get stuck in this trap, we provide some of the best possible preparation for their success. There's no right way to do this and no wrong way. The question is, what's the most effective learning that can take place right now, which will also support the child becoming his own teacher?

Q: *You've said that things are what they are, not right and not wrong, but how can you compare ice cream to the death penalty?*

A: I can talk about ice cream, which I like or I can talk about the death penalty, which I dislike.

I can go get some ice cream, which sounds like a good idea, right now, or I can tell you why I think the death penalty actually works against the achievement of social harmony. Whether it's ice cream or the Kama Sutra or my best childhood friend or TV or the death penalty, each thing exists on its own. There's really nothing to compare them to unless your mind chooses to do that. When your mind compares things, it does so out of a desire to control and be right.

Our mind chooses to compare things all the time. Am I richer than Tina? Am I more handsome than Bob? Am I smarter than my teacher? And so on. What's to be gained by this? If my answer is that I'm smarter, richer, more handsome, etc., does that make me right? If my answer is that I'm not as rich, smart or handsome, does that make me wrong? What am I going to do with my rightness or wrongness? Do I get to cash it in for the ultimate dream vacation or entry into heaven or am I only reinforcing and strengthening my mind's ability to run the show?

We don't even need other people to make these comparisons. We have ourselves to bounce off of. If I think I'm good in one area but not in others, then I can also use that to be hard on myself. "I make good money. How come I can't find a relationship?" "I'm good with people. Why do I have trouble supporting myself?" "I do okay in all the other areas of my life. Why is my health so poor?" On the surface, these seem like reasonable questions. But these comparisons make no sense. What does your ability to earn money have to do with intimacy? Our mind makes these incomparable comparisons simply out of its need to maintain the appearance that we have control.

It's not like we make one comparison and then we're done. Just because I decide that, today, I'm smart and right (We'd be doing good if the feeling lasted a whole day!) doesn't mean I'll feel smart tomorrow or forever. Very quickly, some situation will come along and, once again, I'll be not smart enough and wrong. Comparisons just go on and on because our minds never stop making them.

When we begin to see ourselves and the things in our world as they are, without comparison and without judgment, then we start to weaken our mind's control. New choices and opportunities become evident because we truly desire and feel drawn to them. We begin to move in the direction of life purpose.

3

MEANING

I know what you really think

As infants, our learning is meaningless; we don't make or look for a meaning as to how our eyes move, whether or not we're breast-fed, what our mother looks like, how far our crib is from the window, what color the room is, etc. We don't even assign meanings to what adults call developmental milestones: starting to eat solid food, being able to hold onto a ball, learning that the doll doesn't disappear when it's hidden, crawling, standing, using the toilet and the like. We don't assign meaning but we do feel discomfort or pleasure. That's what drives us, as well as a brain that's designed to learn. If something feels good, we do it again. If it doesn't feel good, we don't. If our brain is being stimulated by what we're doing, we do it more.

While we're engaged in all this wonderfully meaningless exploration and development, our world is responding to us by giving us feedback. The big people have thoughts and feelings and expectations and values about all this stuff. To them, it's anything but meaningless. To them it means that their parenting is right or wrong or you're smart or slow or a good boy or a bad girl. At a certain point, we begin to pay attention to their meanings, even though we still don't have any of our own. And that's when it starts to get messy. If mom is smiling and telling me that I'm a good boy for using the toilet, well, I'm going to pay attention to that. I don't feel any difference between peeing in the toilet and peeing in my diaper. Actually, I have to delay the pleasure of peeing in order to get to the toilet. But my using the toilet gives her pleasure and I want her to care about me so that I'll be taken care of. Our minds are focused on doing everything necessary for our survival. So, we're going to pay a lot of attention to whatever makes the big people happy, upset, angry, sad, etc. Our mind is going to register and record what the big people's feelings, energy and body are telling us about what we're doing.

As we grow to become toddlers and children, we pay an ever-increasing amount of attention to the feedback that the big people give us and we start to focus more on the words. When they're interacting directly with us, we know it's about us and we pay a lot of attention to their feelings and words. Even when they're just nearby, talking with each other, we pay attention because, after all, we are the center of the world and we need to know everything that's going on to ensure our well-being, so we still think it's all about us. We pay attention because our survival depends on it and because our predisposition for learning causes us to take in volumes of information at an age when we are not able to separate what is ours from what is theirs. We listen and feel and start to attach the big people's feelings and meanings to ourselves to ensure that we please them.

So when mom comes home and isn't smiling at me, well then, I must have done something to displease her. What do I, at age two, know about having "a bad hair day?" I make her behavior mean something about me so that I have some chance to control it. If it's not about me, then I have no hope of changing it. This process of making everything mean something about us becomes deeply programmed, deeper than habit, because we're sure our survival depends on it. It becomes so ingrained that we can't recognize that it's taking place.

This programming becomes the pattern of a lifetime. "Dad was drinking at the bar until late. He must not want to read me a bedtime story." "My teacher yelled at the boy next to me in class. She doesn't like him so I better not be friends with him or she won't like me." "The store clerk was rude. What did I do wrong? I must not have been patient enough." "My sister isn't coming to Thanksgiving dinner at my house. She must be mad at me." "My boss didn't smile at me today when he walked by my office. He must not like that report I did." And on and on and on. Many of these examples sound plausible. There's just one big, gigantic, humongous difficulty with taking them at face value. It's not about you! You simply don't know why dad drinks, why the store clerk was rude, why your boss didn't smile, etc. Your mind automatically takes it as a given that it's about you in order to have a chance to control it but that doesn't make it true. It's not about you is a shorthand way of saying that what happened has no inherent meaning about you, and any meaning that you think is there is solely due to your mind's interpretation.

Even if the other person says it's about you, it's still not about you. Let's say your sister tells you that she isn't coming to dinner because she doesn't like the way you set the table or the food you serve or your cooking or the way your children behave. All of these things sure sound like they're about you, don't they? Well, they're not. They're about her. They're her values, her preferences, her beliefs, her opinions. Of course, you could change everything to please her or you could try, anyway, but then you'd be living her life, not yours. Maybe your boss is actually upset about the report you wrote. Maybe he thinks you didn't do a very good job. It's still not about you. It's his opinion, his values, etc. You may choose to change the way you do reports in the future but that doesn't mean you're wrong or bad or stupid or a poor employee. It's not about you. You see, if you make it about you, if you make all of these other people's opinions and behaviors mean something about you, you eliminate your ability to discover who you are outside of their beliefs about who you should be. Instead of learning about your gifts, your strengths, your likes and dislikes, you'll spend your entire life trying to please other people and, strangely enough, not succeeding. Sound familiar?

As children, we needed to make everything about us so that we could please the big people, in order to survive. As adults, we're still trying to get others to believe that what we think and feel is about them so that we can control them. They're still trying to get us to believe that what they think and feel is about us so that they can control us. Control is not bad or evil, it's just what we've learned to do to survive. How much more of your life do you want to spend trying to read other people's minds so that, just maybe, you can meet their expectations? And, if you actually succeed in being who they want you to be, is that going to make it easier or harder to be yourself in the future?

The tricky part about meaning is that it's not about whatever thing we appear to be discussing. When I say "War is bad" or "John's a good student" or "This is a hard chair," it appears that I'm talking about a specific person or thing. Actually, though, I'm only expressing my meaning assignments and judgments about those things. In other words, I'm talking about me! When we see this clearly, it's apparent that most misunderstandings occur because two or more people think they're talking about the same objectified thing and each one is really talking about themselves. Because what others say or do is not about you, doesn't mean you're not going to have feelings about it. Most of the time, our feelings about the ways others react toward us are based on our making it mean something bad or wrong. You may be upset when you find that what you do is not always liked, appreciated, accepted, etc. You may feel sad when you realize how much of your life has already been used trying to please others or reacting to what others do, when it's not even about you. You may laugh when you understand how much of our time is spent in such a silly way.

It works the same for desirable things, as well. "The boss smiled at me today. He likes the way I'm dressing." "The professor complimented my homework. I'll bet I'm getting an A." "The waitress was really pleasant. She must know I'm a big tipper." "He sent me a beautiful bouquet of roses. He's going to propose this weekend." Again, you don't know why your boss smiled or why the waitress was pleasant or that you're getting an A. These people's behaviors are not about you. If you make them about you, you may have some unpleasant awakenings when your predictions don't come true or you find out that the meanings you assigned are not valid. Actually, it's worse than that. When you realize that the meanings you assigned were incorrect, your mind, working the way it does, is going to tell you that you're stupid or slow or wrong or bad for not figuring out what was really going on. It's going to assign an additional meaning to your mistake and you're going to make that about you, as well.

It would be troublesome enough if we only made other people's behaviors, beliefs and opinions about us. The worst part is that we continually make our own stuff mean something about us. We're with ourselves much more than we're with others so our mind has never-ending opportunities to assign all kinds of meanings, mostly negative, to our thoughts and behaviors. All these meaning assignments are a product of our mind's desire to control. They are reduced, by our mind, to good or bad. You're either good or bad, depending on your reading of the other person's behavior and speech or your judgments about yourself. If you make it about you, then every time you decide you're good, you're going to be on guard against anything that makes you think you're bad. If you decide that it means you're bad, well, now you'll have to figure out what to do so you can be good again. Like right and wrong, this is a roller coaster with lots of thrills, chills, ups and downs that runs in a loop and leaves you back at the beginning wondering where to go for your next ride. Roller coasters can be great fun, they're just not known for helping us to develop and grow. If the ride is enjoyable, go ahead. If it's not fun anymore, maybe there's another choice.

We continually assign meaning based on historical conditioning of which we are unaware. We assign meanings to things, behaviors, and feelings. Then, the judgment usually follows. Let's say I'm talking on the phone with my father and I speak curtly to him. I assign the meaning that I did something bad. Then I label that behavior as wrong. So now, I'm wrong and therefore unloved. I get off the phone feeling inadequate, at best. The next time we talk, I'm on guard against saying the wrong thing, so I don't express myself, and I can only speak from a tight, contracted place, which feels effortful and tiring. Soon, maybe I start to believe that life would be easier if I just didn't talk to him! Until we interrupt the cycle and recognize, in the moment, our state of limitation and contraction, we can only repeat similar variations of this scenario.

There are other ways that our mind uses to keep things simple and controllable. Categories and labels may not sound the same as meanings, yet they function, for our mind, in the same way. Look at the category of things we call books. The dictionary says that a book is a set of written, printed or blank sheets bound into a volume. Is it still called a book when I print out these pages on loose sheets of paper and send them to the publisher? How about if I put it all on a computer disk? What if you read it on the Internet or hear it on an audiotape? Actually, most people would agree that these are all forms of the things we call books, because we have expanded our concept of what we include in this category. What about the category of love? Does love from a child fit? How about love from a student? What about a pet? How about a stranger? How about my love for chocolate? Maybe the source doesn't matter as much as the qualities. Is it love if it's conditional? Is it love if you never see each other again? Is it love while you fight? What about the categories of friendship, compassion, patience, self-trust? There's hardly any category we can come up with that doesn't have at least several exceptions our minds will identify.

Our mind creates categories and then continually judges whether something fits into that category or doesn't. This makes sense. It aids survival. Metal is not in most of our categories of food as it doesn't provide useful nourishment. Walking across the freeway at rush hour is not in most of our categories of safety. The tricky part is that our mind automatically excludes things from its categories without giving us the chance to think and feel about whether we want to include them. Suppose my brother turns me down for a loan, but my friend gives me the money. Does this mean my brother doesn't love me and my friend does? That may well be the meaning my mind assigns to this. Does that make it true?

Where this becomes even more important is in the category of things we label as healing and learning. How often do we not hear valuable information because we have put it in the "I already know that" category? How many times do we exclude something because it falls into the "unreliable source" category? Then there's the "That won't work for me" category, the "Prove it to me first" category, the "He's a charlatan" category, etc. When your mind filters out information, it doesn't ask your permission. It simply ignores it as if it didn't exist. Does that mean you should take in and accept everything from every source? No. Perhaps a better question is to ask how you can begin to catch your mind in the act of filtering and excluding useful information. You may be surprised to find how often you've been doing it and, consequently, missing out on opportunities for growth.

Our minds simplify all the possible meanings into good or bad in order to control. "I got a raise, so I'm good." "I got a speeding ticket, so I'm bad." What our mind does with good is use it as a temporary vindication. What it does with bad is turn it into a source of shame, guilt, and embarrassment. To our minds, it's life and death, something we have to repeat, fix, solve, cure or eradicate. As with the judgment of right and wrong, our mind's action of assigning meaning is what lets you know that it's hard at work, managing anything and everything that it believes must be controlled.

Assigning meaning diverts our energy into doing things other than following our true desires and preferences. Maybe you can't please mom, though you've never stopped trying and you can't seem to fix that part of yourself that, you believe, makes her not love you. Okay, you've been working on this for 30 years now. What part of you is still trying to fix something that takes so much energy while also having such a low probability of success? Maybe it's only your mind that forever makes mom's behavior mean there's something wrong with you. Maybe it's only your mind that keeps telling you you've got to fix this one or die trying!

* * *

Q: *How can I tell when I'm making what someone else says or does mean something about me?*

A: It's challenging, sometimes, to be able to tell when we are operating like puppets with our mind pulling the strings. Our mind doesn't want us to be able to easily identify when it's working. Remember, it always tries to operate as if the puppet show were running itself. Our mind wants to stay hidden and behind the scenes.

One way is to check for emotional charges or feelings that don't really apply to what is going on. Feeling like you want to run away and hide, when someone is talking, is usually an indication that your mind is saying it's about you and it's not good. Or, you may be feeling justified, validated or vindicated if you've accepted your mind's interpretation that it's about you and you're right. Either way, there's going to be some feeling, which is a reflection of the assigned meaning, which really has nothing to do with what's being said.

When a friend or stranger gives you a compliment, how do you react? Do you agree, disagree, get flustered, ask them what they mean? What about when a friend or stranger puts you down? Is that easier or harder to let in? How come? What's our mind's role in this? Unfortunately, out of our mind's desire to control, we attach meanings, which often have nothing to do with the intention of the sender. Human conversation is an ongoing example of this. One of the things we get as a byproduct of assigning meaning is that we get to feel shame, guilt, remorse, regret, righteousness, superiority and so on. It's another way our mind reminds us it's there.

You could also imagine how you would feel if your mind weren't talking. There is a feeling of ease and relaxation, which accompanies taking in information without it meaning anything about you. We're unfamiliar with the feeling of not scrambling to figure out what everything means. It takes some time to identify it and become comfortable with it. It's the feeling that happens when we have some vague notion that we should be doing something, while at the same time realizing there's nothing to do because everything is okay just the way it is.

Recognizing the "there's nothing to do" feeling becomes a huge relief when we look back on all those times that we reacted out of our mind's fear that we had to do something to fix the situation, solve the problem, blame someone, apologize, pretend, deny or whatever our mind brought up. We're so busy trying to fix things all the time, in reaction to all the judgments and meanings, that we don't know what to do when there's nothing to do, yet our mind keeps shouting that we have to do something!

A further way to tell that we've gotten sucked up in another round of the meaning game is that we become defensive. Did you ever wonder why we often get defensive when we hear information we don't like? Will we die if we don't defend ourselves? Will we lose our position in the human race? Will we never be able to show our face in public again? Yes, if you believe your mind. Our mind says that our survival is threatened and since we don't want to admit an error, as that would mean we're wrong, bad, etc., the best thing to do is to pretend it didn't happen, deny it or attack the other person.

Our language is also a big clue to our mind's operations. We often use words or phrases such as "have to," "should" and "must." I have to get up and go to work, call my mom, buy a card for Jean's birthday, mow the lawn, pick up the kids, etc., etc., etc. Our minds have a never-ending supply of obligations for us to continually fulfill or risk feeling guilty. What if each one of these obligations was a choice? How would that change our feelings about them?

Adults, that is, people who have reached a level of independent functioning such that they are free from most of their mind's strategies, don't "have to" do anything. Now, your mind may think that means they just live their lives in some chaotic, irresponsible way. Actually, adults feel and welcome the responsibilities they have chosen such that they rarely feel a sense of obligation. Children and big people functioning like children, feel they "have to" do things to survive. This is another example of how, what we started out doing made sense at the time and is now continued, even when it no longer applies.

Projection is yet another way we can tell that we've fallen into the meaning trap. When we've made some aspect of ourselves unacceptable, because of the meaning we've assigned, our mind must find a way to deal with it. Let's say I've made my procrastination mean that I'm not a good person. I will want to avoid acknowledging this apparent shortcoming because every time I do, I will also be faced with my feelings of not being good enough. So what am I going to do when I see what I interpret as someone else's procrastination? Ignore it? Hah! Not hardly. I'm going to use the opportunity to disassociate myself even further from my unacceptable part, by pointing the finger at someone else. I'm going to harshly point out his/her procrastination as a way of saying, in effect, here's something that you're wrong or bad for that I'm not. I'm going to "project" my unacceptable part and all its associated meanings onto them in the hope of getting myself to believe that I'm okay. Does this work? Well, our mind keeps doing it so it does offer some kind of, at least, momentary relief. It's like not putting weight on a broken leg. You get some temporary pain reduction but without the other steps needed for healing. We'll continue to do it as long as that's the only way we can feel better.

Projection works another way as well. Suppose I really love to cook but I got the message somewhere and believed it, that cooking isn't manly or that I don't do it very well or I should find a better way to spend my time. When I find someone who has given themselves more permission than me, in this area, I'm likely to project onto them how wonderful they and their cooking are. I'm going to take that part of me that I like and have shut off and use this indirect way of acknowledging and appreciating it. Most of us have at least one projection about a part of ourselves we've decided is faulty and at least one about an aspect that we like but lacks permission. They come down to the same thing. We project what is unacceptable.

Q: *You've said the worst part about meaning is when we make our own mistakes mean something about us. How can they not? Aren't our own mistakes a reflection of who we are?*

A: Yes, that's what makes it difficult. You'd think that if you make an error, well of course that's a direct reflection of you. Yet, this is still your mind wanting to exert control. So I forget my girlfriend's birthday or I get lost on the way to the theater because I didn't call for directions, or whatever. Therefore, I'm bad, wrong, stupid, uncaring, neglectful, etc., etc. Pick whatever situation and meaning you like. Where do those meanings come from? Was I born with a meaning assigned to each and every one of the possible things I may do in this lifetime? Not very likely. Those meanings are learned from our experiences and the others involved in them and, thereafter, we continue to assign those meanings to every similar situation. How does that change? Am I forever doomed to beat myself up every time I make a mistake? That's the implication of meanings. You're stuck with them until you change them. So, after a lifetime of this are you ready to change? What would that look like?

One way it might look different is if, somehow, a mistake was simply a mistake, an error was merely an error. In other words, it didn't mean anything about you. This challenges our mind's basic mechanisms of control. If our mind can't make it mean something, then it can't control it. Our mind has got to, at least, make things right or wrong, good or bad. Without that, well, our mind is just screwed! It might as well give up and go fishing. And that's the point. That's what we want.

We want our mind to say, in effect, "Well, if this guy won't even acknowledge that he's a dummy when he makes a mistake, then he's hopeless, I give up trying to fix him."

Changing the programming that we have from childhood and all the repeated experiences, afterwards, requires that we are vigilant in catching our mind assigning meanings. It usually takes a number of successes, catching our mind doing it's meaning dance, before we're able to laugh at ourselves about this. That's another way that things look different. Many people, when they start to not assign meaning, get a clearer picture of how often they used to do it. When they feel the blessed silence of their mind not talking, they are often filled with laughter. Sometimes it's sadness at all the lost years and pain they've caused themselves and others but often it's simply laughter. Laughter at how deeply our programming runs. Laughter at how silly we can be. Laughter at the human drama.

My mistakes don't mean anything about me unless my mind remains in control. And, consequently, my successes, also, don't mean anything about me unless I choose to believe what my mind is telling me. Most people find that this change leaves them with an almost unimaginable amount of freedom to be who they are, to like what they like, to follow their preferences and desires, to say yes and no easily, and perhaps, surprisingly, to take full responsibility for their lives.

Lots of people, hearing the idea that things have no inherent meaning, get very scared and reactive. They think this means (there it is again) that this will result in a world of chaos where everyone gets to do exactly what they want because they're no longer constrained by what they've learned about right and wrong, good and bad, etc. That fear is their mind once again trying to exert control. Their mind doesn't do that because it really fears a world of chaos—it does that because it fears being out of work! Our mind freely and repeatedly confuses choice and requirement, meaning and value, obligation and responsibility.

True responsibility is a feeling that grows out of choice. We choose to be responsible when we are not always so busy trying to please and control others. Obligation is resented responsibility. It's resented because it has not been freely chosen.

So, another way that things look different, without a world of assigned meanings, is that we all start to act more responsibly. Not because it's the law, or the rule or we've been told to or it's the right thing to do. Rather, because responsibility is a natural outcome of both genuinely feeling our present condition and the desire to help others move in the same direction. And, since one of the most powerful ways of learning new skills and abilities is teaching others, not only do we get to further enhance what we are learning, but those people we care about benefit, as well.

4

MISPERCEPTION

*Calling it the way I see it,
even if my eyes are closed*

How is it that we learn to hear, see, taste, touch, move, feel, think? Did someone teach us how to do these things? Research is revealing that the neuromuscular development, timing and organization required to do a seemingly simple function like walking is so complicated that we're still at the very beginning of helping to restore this ability to people that have lost it. If walking is that complex, imagine what our brains are doing when involved in functions such as recognition, memory, recall, imagination and dreams.

One of the attributes that most other mammals have in common is that they come into the world with the largest part of their brain prewired for all the essential tasks needed to survive and reproduce. We, however, are born with most of our brain unprogrammed and available for learning new information, well beyond what is needed for survival and reproduction. We have a long developmental period before we can even feed ourselves and a lot of blank space, if you will, in our brains, waiting to be filled with a vast amount of data, concepts, imagery, thoughts, emotions, etc.

The learning we do in the first three years of life creates the foundation upon which all future learning and behavior is based, including use of our senses, the recognition and feeling of emotion, the capacity for intimacy, the development of identity and the ability to think. The tools we use for learning, for taking in information, are the various modes of perception that we have available. Initially, we have the ability to hear, see, touch, taste and smell. We also have some abilities, which, while not commonly thought of as avenues of perception, are essential to our knowledge of ourselves and the world. These include movement, learning, kinesthesia (the ability to feel where the parts of our body are in space), proprioception (the ability to feel our own internal stimuli) and intuition. These tools create a perceptual network by which we orient ourselves, identify things, stay safe and learn more about our surroundings, ourselves and others.

More than any other creatures, we are created in such a way that our capacity for learning seems unlimited. We are like learning machines. While the number of brain cells we have is finite, the number of possible connections between them is calculated to be greater than all the atoms in the universe—essentially infinite. Our mind develops after our brain has already been working for a while. Our mind comes to the party after our body and brain have already become grounded in the physical plane. This is another reason why our mind works so hard at solving problems, fixing things, controlling whatever it can. Our mind has to figure out what the heck is going on, who the players are and who's hiding the rulebook, without the advantage of having been around from the start. So while our mind wants to fix the past, to undo all those bad and wrong things we must have done to end up where we are, it also wants to predict the future, to make sure whatever we did doesn't happen again. Running around in circles, in this way, leads our mind to operate like it's a couple of steps behind, which it is.

It's also out of step because after using our senses to perceive, it has to filter out the unwanted information, which is anything that would threaten its control, then it has to categorize what kind of threat there is, then search for the closest similar situation in the past and, finally, it can respond. All this happens rather quickly, but as you start to pay more attention to your mind's operations, you can begin to recognize the tiny hesitations and the processing taking place. It often feels like there's no delay because we're so practiced at quickly reacting, defending, blaming, judging, etc.

Because our mind is out of step it relies almost exclusively on information, based on the past, which it has altered to meet its needs. As infants, we initially had no sense of time. We simply sensed that things lasted until they changed. A baby can cry for hours because it's stuck in the feeling of discomfort and sees no end in sight. It's also why children cry so easily and long at what we experience as insignificant. They initially have no idea that the toy will be found or that mom is coming back. And, it's why, when we experience physical and emotional pain, we get so frustrated or depressed about it. Physical or emotional pain can take us straight back in time to those early experiences when the pain went on, seemingly forever.

Most of us have heard the saying "This too, shall pass," yet we have an awfully hard time remembering it when we're in the middle of pain. Fear and pain seem to be the quickest ways that our mind travels back to the past in order to come up with a previous solution to the currently imagined problem. And, our mind doesn't like to travel without company. The rest of who we are willingly goes along for the ride, until we learn how to recognize what has happened and bring ourselves back to the present.

Because our mind does not operate in the present, it spends a lot of time trying to predict the future. Predicting the future is one of the things our mind does best, though not very well. After all, the data it uses are a lot of experiences that have been highly filtered and altered and assigned meanings based on our mind's model of the world, not on what was true in the past and definitely not on what is happening now. Our mind co-opts our senses to maintain its model. It turns yes into no and no into yes. It turns statements into questions and observations into judgments. It inserts words into the other person's mouth. It puts cotton in our ears and filters over our eyes. In short, our mind transforms any information that threatens its control, especially what we see and hear.

Many studies have been done showing that we all tend to see and hear events differently. Besides being a reflection of our varying capacities for observation, memory and recall, it also shows how much our mind controls what information is excluded, what is included and what is altered. Genetics, culture and upbringing are all factors in this, yet the single biggest influence over how we filter information is the many ways in which our minds reinforce their particular models by using habitual solutions to the problems they identify.

Our mind uses our perceptual senses to help it assign meaning to events as part of its need to identify cause and effect. Our mind must identify a cause and effect relationship in order to control. If it can identify the cause and the effect, then it can try to minimize or enhance the cause, depending on the desired outcome. Like the many other ways that it works, our mind exerts the most control over those aspects of our behavior which are more hidden. That way, we're much less likely to catch our mind doing its dance.

Cause and effect is one of those tricky things that we think we understand but often get confused. If I hold a ball in my hand and drop it, what was the cause? That I opened my fingers or gravity? If I give you a compliment and you are pleased, was the cause that I smiled or the words I used or that you heard it in a way that gave you pleasure or all of these? If your romantic relationships often fail, is it because you're afraid of commitment, didn't have a good model for intimate relationship when growing up, always seem to pick the wrong person, or any of a number of possible "causes"?

Cause and effect does exist. It's our mind's predictive control of it that leads us to misperceive what's happening. In this way, it can maintain the illusions that are so fundamental to its continued operation. How could our mind justify all of its actions if it didn't believe that it controls the future by taking certain actions in the present? In other words, why would I try to please you (cause) so that you'll love me (effect) if I have no reason to believe that you'll be pleased by my actions? How would we explain our lives if we didn't believe that what happened in our past caused us to be who we are now? What if the hurtful memories of your life weren't actually caused by things that happened in the past? What if you really have no ability to predict the future based on things you're doing now? What if cause and effect, in the way our mind uses it, is simply a story to convince us that there really is such a thing as control? The implications of not using cause and effect as a justification or explanation for our behavior are so far reaching that we rarely even consider them. Our mind must use cause and effect as its rationale for control or the whole game is over, which, when you begin to recognize your mind at work, it is.

Our mind, understandably, doesn't want to accept that, in the realm of perception, interpretation and response, which is so much of human behavior, cause and effect is unpredictable and, therefore, uncontrollable. Yet, when we let go of our mind, our experience tells us that this is the case. Pick any emotionally charged experience from your past and identify at least one assumption you made or meaning you assigned to yourself or the other person about why that experience happened. Cause and effect just flew out the window. Pick any experience where the actual outcome was significantly different than what you intended. Where's the cause and effect now? You might be saying that these are the exceptions and that, most of the time, things work out as expected. Yes it does appear that way. But given how much our minds like rules and certainty, we might be more than a little suspicious about its ability to easily discount any exceptions. Additionally, we tend to have some unspoken agreements with each other such as not letting ourselves know how we feel, not telling others how we feel and, in general, not making a "big deal" out of things. You know; be cool, get along, don't sweat the small stuff, etc. Isn't that what we were taught as children? So, while it appears that cause and effect is a reliable and controllable relationship, it's our mind that must believe this and will alter and interpret events accordingly.

Our mind is the only part of us convinced that the weird and silly things we believe and often do in relationship to ourselves and others, make any sense, whatsoever. What would we do in a world where we're not trying to please others because we have no belief that they're going to take care of us, in return? We would do what we like, discover our life purpose, follow our own lead. Our minds simply can't allow that. To our minds, that possibility is too unpredictable, too scary and perhaps worst of all, there's no guarantee of success.

Our mind is the child that each of us is still raising. It needs our compassion, support and our adult capacity to clarify what's going on in the present as opposed to what happened in the past, which didn't really happen as we remember it, only our filtered and highly processed version of it. It's similar to becoming so used to processed food that we become doubtful that it's okay to eat it in its natural, raw state. What would an experience be in its raw state? Well, what would it be like to have a loved one yell at you in anger and for you to experience that without your mind making them wrong, making yourself wrong, without defending, shrinking or running away? That might be quite difficult to imagine, especially given our mind's habitual reactions to situations like this. You might even doubt that it's possible at all.

What we call experience is, more often than not, our mind's version of what happened. When some teachers talk about the great illusion, this is what they are referring to. Our mind goes through its dance routine of misperceptions, judgments, meanings, etc. and labels that the experience. In short, we do not experience the event; we experience our mind. An experience, without our mind's intervention, is simply the event with no meaning, judgment, interpretation or alteration.

Our response to events, when our mind is quiet, is felt as someplace along the continuum from pleasure to pain. We liked it, disliked it or are neutral about it and, however we feel, there are no judgments. It didn't mean anything about us or the other person then or now. This is not the same as not having feelings about it. Actually, without all our mind's stuff going on, it's so much easier to clearly recognize how we feel about each experience.

Perception is tricky because we rarely question it. Due to our mind's insistence on its view of reality and its position as the center of the universe, we also assume that others experience the world the same way we do. This assumption is the basis for many of our misunderstandings and miscommunications. Take the words, "I love you." Your mind's interpretation may be, "Love means that you'll do what I ask, never leave me and never hurt me. And, because you love me, you'll behave as I've predicted." Doesn't quite work that way, does it? It's not only that my perceptions and beliefs don't quite match yours. I never checked them out with you, so when the bubble breaks, I'm likely to be angry, disappointed, sad, frustrated, etc.

Perception is also tricky because we don't know what we don't know. Yes, we can acknowledge that we don't know the capital of every country in the world or the distance from the Sun to Pluto or all of the proteins in our body but those are not things our mind needs to know in order to maintain control. Our mind doesn't willingly recognize how often we get in our own way because that's too close to home, too close to our mind's area of operation. Our mind must at least pretend to know everything that is relevant to what it does, otherwise, it would have to continually question what it's doing and become immobilized. So we pretend, a lot. Similarly, our mind will deny the existence of certain information, which, if acknowledged, would threaten its very existence. So we deny, a lot. These processes of pretense and denial are carried on in response to perceptions, which would otherwise change our habitual behaviors, with our mind shrinking significantly as a direct consequence.

* * *

Q: *How can I know when I'm accurately perceiving what is going on around me?*

A: Probably the easiest way is to sense your response. Did you have a knee-jerk reaction? That's a pretty good clue that you perceived a threat in the environment that may not be there. Our minds are particularly attuned to any kind of perceptual information that signals some kind of threat around us. It's usually not a threat to our physical well-being but our mind perceives it that way and quickly reacts.

Another way would be to get everyone else to agree with your perceptions so the question of accuracy becomes irrelevant. That's the approach that our mind often uses, without much success, though it does help to explain how mobs and cults operate. Unless we all agree to appoint some King of Reality (your mind already has that job) and also agree to follow his/her dictates, it's very unlikely that we're all going to have the same perceptions all the time.

Wanting to be sure that you're perceiving accurately is not too far from wanting to be right, a cue that your mind may be running the show. Your perceptions are just that, your perceptions: not hers, not his, not mine, not theirs. They're not right and not wrong. Perceptual accuracy has a lot to do with your intention and desire. If your desire is to use information to grow and evolve, this will involve questioning, rather than doubting, what you think and feel in a way that supports growth. Questions that are simply an exploration of your nature tend to be in the form of, "What am I experiencing?" or "What is this?" Whereas, questions reflecting doubt often appear in the form of "Am I doing the right thing?" or "Is my behavior justified?" or "What does this mean about me?"

As we begin to evolve, we develop self-trust and start to doubt ourselves less frequently. Let's say that I'm listening to a political candidate deliver a speech and I observe that everyone seems to be nodding their heads occasionally, in apparent agreement with everything he's saying. My experience, though, is that I sense incongruity between his words, body language and energy. Will I trust the accuracy of my perceptions or will I doubt them? I could ask others in the crowd if they shared my perception. If they say no, do I diminish myself because of it? If they say yes, do I enlarge myself as a result? Here's a simple test. If, when I have my perceptions, they are accompanied by a judgment about the rightness or wrongness of what I'm observing, then my perceptions are probably not accurate. If there is a judgment involved or meaning assigned, my mind is active and I have projected myself into the situation in a way that precludes reliable perception.

Perceptual accuracy involves the ability to sense on several levels. It's holding in consciousness the present environment and people, the interactions taking place and the judgments, meanings and strategies employed by yourself and others, in an effort to control what is happening. Another way to look at it is that accurate perception includes awareness of everything happening on the surface and below the surface, at the same time.

When you look at the cluttered garage that you've been meaning to clean up for quite a while now, do you also perceive how you may be judging yourself for not already having done it? And, most importantly, do you perceive that there is no connection between the cluttered garage and your judgment about it, other than what your mind has created in order to control? Like other areas, this is not black and white. Perceptual ability expands as you give up control and develop more permission, acceptance and self-trust.

One of our most valuable perceptual tools is intuition. It's not based on any hard information; we simply feel something and then choose how to act upon it. We often don't use it because our mind doubts its value, doubts that it can be relied upon. Well, you can't rely on your mind either so you might as well give intuition a try. Intuition can tell us to turn in a certain direction when we're lost or disoriented. It can tell us whether someone wants their pain to be touched or left alone. It can direct us to speak or be silent. Developing intuition requires permission and self-trust. If you wait until you think you'll be right every time before you act, it will take a very long time to trust your intuition. Intuition is like the rest of our body. It grows stronger and more reliable with use and atrophies when not employed. We don't stop using a hand because it occasionally drops the glass.

5

STRATEGIES

*If I can't run away,
at least I can make you scared, too*

Our mind continually misses the boat. It can't be in the present because it has to rely on our senses to first receive the information. Then it has to filter out the parts that don't fit its preexisting model, process it, figure out who's right and wrong, good and bad, decide what problem has to be solved to control the situation and, only then, can it come up with some response or strategy, which will also miss the boat since the strategy is usually a repetition of some previous behavior done to ward off a perceived threat, which no longer exists though our mind is convinced it does. Sound convoluted or confusing? Yes, much of what we do, especially in relationships, is often inexplicable to ourselves and nonsensical or humorous to others.

In order for our mind to search for a suitable response, it reviews what has worked before. Time travel is not science fiction. We do it all the time. Our mind is the vehicle we use. Whenever our mind perceives a threat, it takes us back in time to what we did when we originally felt that threat and then responds in a very similar way. It does this out of programming and habit. Our mind, out of fear, simply reaches for the quickest way to defend itself and maintain some, hoped for, control of the situation. And the quickest response is going to be something that it's already used. It doesn't matter to our mind that this response doesn't work that well anymore or that the situation is different or that the people are different. Unfortunately, with this kind of time travel, we rarely recognize what has happened. We're simply operating as if we're one or three or seven or whatever age the original strategy developed.

Strategies are a device that our mind uses, a preconceived solution to a problem of human interaction that our mind has identified. For example, if you yell at me, and that makes me afraid that I've done something wrong, I may tell you how bad or guilty or ashamed I feel in the hope that you'll stop being mad at me and we won't have to talk about it any more. That's a strategy. I did it in the past. It worked at least once, or I thought it did. It sort of still works, due to my mind's denial of what's really going on, so I'm going to keep on using it because it's quick and easy and I don't have to feel or think or take responsibility. A strategy is a responsibility avoidance mechanism.

Sometimes we develop fairly intricate and complex strategies but most of the time we use the same tried and true methods. Take forgiveness, as an example. Did you ever wonder why we don't forgive certain hurts easily, why we seem to hang on to things and develop grudges? What would be the possible benefits, for us, of withholding forgiveness? None. There aren't any. So, what part of us is still holding out? Oh yeah, it's our mind and it can come up with lots of seemingly rational reasons for doing really silly things. What does our mind tell us are good reasons for withholding forgiveness? Well, how about, "He's wrong so why should I forgive him?" This one won't change until we find a way to get free of the right/wrong trap. "She hasn't admitted it's her fault" or "She hasn't apologized" or "She hasn't made it up to me." These mildly disguised versions of the right/wrong trap are sometimes referred to as the "pound of flesh" theory of forgiveness. You're waiting for the other person to, first, pay their penance and then, maybe, you'll forgive them. "Why should I be the one to act first?" "They should come to me" or "If I apologize, they'll think it was all my fault." These are other disguises for right/wrong thinking, as well as a fear of being perceived as weak. There are more versions of this but the point is that we don't see forgiveness as an opportunity for healing and growth. Our mind uses it only as a further way to keep chewing the fat of right and wrong, hoping that eventually we'll be vindicated.

Our mind also holds on to not forgiving because it uses grudges like emotional nourishment. Long withheld forgiveness starts to take on a life of its own. "My mom really messed me up" or "My dad never supported me" become like mantras that our mind dwells on and draws strength from, especially when we recognize some kind of problem or lack in our lives. "Job troubles—what do you expect—you should see my father." "Relationship difficulties—you never met my first three husbands." "Health problems—of course—look at my childhood." What better than something that happened years or decades ago, can't be changed and sounds so justified? Who could blame or think less of us?

It's not that our histories aren't important for understanding who we are, it's that we have the option of using them for our learning and, instead, we tend to use them as excuses for being stuck. Our mind won't let us see the past in a different light because it must hold on to its justification for everything that we've done since then. Forgiveness would require letting go of who we were. Letting go of the past, especially those experiences that we feel have hurt us, could lead to a confusing lack of meaning about our lives and a disturbing amount of choice about our future. So, there are lots of good reasons for not forgiving, at least to our minds.

Asking questions is another, to our mind, useful strategy. What's strategic about asking questions? Most questions are statements in disguise. Remember how much our minds like to remain hidden? Questions are frequently used as a hidden way to express doubt or to tell someone that they're wrong, stupid, don't know what they're talking about, etc. It often sounds like "What about a situation where . . .?" or "How can you be sure that they didn't mean . . .?" or "How does that apply to me?" Not all questions are disguised statements but when you listen to the energy of the question you can often hear the unspoken statement behind it. Why would our mind not want us to simply make a statement? Because our mind believes that by asking a question, instead of making a statement, it can control the fear of being wrong.

Take a common relationship situation where two or more people are deciding what to do for fun. "What do you want to do?" "I don't know. What do you want to do?" This often becomes a routine, playing the "What do you want to do?" game. How would the game change if we simply said what we would like, instead? "I'd like to stay home tonight and read a book" is a risky thing to say when you want to please the other person. Maybe they want to go to a movie or to dance. Maybe their response is, "Okay, we'll stay home" and you can feel their disappointment. Maybe their response is, "Well, you stay home if you want but I'm going out" and you can feel their anger. Maybe their response is, "I always do what you want" and you can feel their frustration. Why risk having to deal with any one of these when you can avoid it all by asking a question and, with neither one of you taking full responsibility for what you want, things will work out in a, sort of, mutually unsatisfactory way! Questions are safer than statements, we believe, because they avoid the responsibility of identifying and acting on our desires and they reduce the risk of unpleasant feelings when our desires don't agree with the other person's.

Another unfortunate use of questions is the "Why are you crying?" or "Why are you angry?" type of question. These kinds of questions are also disguised statements. We ask these kinds of questions when we're afraid of the expression of strong emotion, because of what we make it mean about us, and we want to avoid that possibility by attempting to turn it back on the other person. If we can make the other person feel doubt about their emotions or the way they're expressing their feelings, we can avoid having to hear something that we fear. These kinds of questions are often heard as a demand to explain yourself or justify your behavior, which is what children often feel when asked by their parents why they did something their parents think they shouldn't have. We might as well ask, "Why are you feeling?" Were we to make a statement, instead, it might be something like, "I get scared when you cry or get angry because I'm afraid I might have done something wrong." Simply turning it into a statement reveals that our mind is on guard, assigning meaning, judging and looking for a way to control. It's not the words themselves that convey the hidden statement—a mother could certainly ask her daughter why she was crying—it's the energy with which the question is asked.

Statements are risky. What's the risk you'd like to avoid more—the other person's hurt feelings or your own? Most of the time, in relationships, we try to prevent the other person's disappointment at the expense of our own well-being. Yet, again, this is our mind's black and white thinking: right/wrong, good/bad, you/me. This is another strategy we often employ; thinking that we're stuck with only two possibilities and neither one is very desirable. It's not in our mind's best interests to see that there are other options or choices. Multiple choices are threatening to our mind because it cannot reduce them to either/or. Too many variables challenge our mind's control. Much of our feeling of stuckness doesn't actually come from a lack of choices. Rather, it's a product of unclear or unstated desires. Whenever you feel stuck, you immediately know that your mind is running the show.

When you and the other person clearly let each other know what you want, the guessing and gaming is eliminated. This is a huge help in reducing anxiety, and it gives the other person something tangible to respond to. Further, by stating your desire, you have implied that they too have permission to do the same. It can also feel like a great relief to no longer be denying what you want or pretending that it doesn't matter. Sometimes it doesn't matter and, then, you can say so, but when it's important, pretending that it's not only adds to the confusion. All of this leads to greater trust in the other person and, more importantly, in yourself. We tend to distrust people who don't clearly state their feelings and desires and, not surprisingly, we tend to distrust ourselves for the same reasons. You may not always like what the other person says but, if they can be direct, you don't doubt that they will take care of themselves. And, if they take care of themselves, by stating their needs, then you don't have to try to read their mind to figure out what to do. If you take care of yourself, in the same way, they don't have to constantly be guessing either. If that sounds like a relief, you may want to give it a try. If it sounds scary, you may want to explore what you're making it mean about you or them.

Stating your desires is freeing, even if they are not realized. Desires that bounce around in our heads or hearts aren't quite real until they are stated out loud. Once they are verbally acknowledged, especially to someone we care about, they take on a life force that greatly increases the likelihood that they will be realized. We're often afraid to do this because our mind can't so easily control what is out in the open. By now, you may be saying that this is all fine and well, but you still have to work to support yourself and your family, you have to pick up your children and take them to soccer practice, you have to get your tax information ready for the accountant, you have to go to Thanksgiving dinner at your mother's house, you have to deal with rush hour traffic and so on.

Be suspicious of these perceived obligations. They are a big clue to your mind's need to control your fear. Get clear and acknowledge, out loud, to someone you care about and who cares about you, what your desire is in regard to this thing where you feel stuck. Is it really true that you "have to" do this? What's the worst case scenario if you don't? How likely is that? What other options are there? Here, it's really helpful to get input from someone who is good at brainstorming, someone who can freely come up with ideas without regard to how practical they are. Often, when we come up with other options, we quickly discount or disregard them because that's another thing our mind does to maintain control and status quo. Carefully consider each option. Instead of figuring out why it won't work, which is your mind's goal, figure out why it will work. Most importantly, after thoroughly examining your stuckness, take responsibility for either continuing what you're already doing or implementing the new choice that you've created.

Being responsible and feeling stuck cannot co-exist. Responsibility is welcoming all of the many possible outcomes of your choices and, this is the tricky part—the part your mind will want to fight to the death—whatever you do is a choice.

Feeling stuck is a way of avoiding the potential of who you are. As fetuses, infants, toddlers and children, our choices were limited. We depended on the big people for almost everything. At a certain point, however, we started to provide those things for ourselves because we're here; we survived. If you still believe that someone is making you do things, how does your mind hand over that power? And if you believe you're making yourself do it, then it's your choice. Either it's a choice or you're going to feel and act like a victim. As much as our mind still tries to convince us, everyday, that our choices are limited, it simply isn't so. It's one of our mind's biggest and most enduring lies. But it's a great way, fully utilized by our mind, of avoiding responsibility.

Qualifiers make a useful strategy. "You don't have to talk about it if you don't want to." *It sounds like you may be more uncomfortable talking about this than me.* "Let me be honest . . ." *What have you been doing up to now? Lying?* "I'm saying this for your own good." *You'd like me to believe that's it's for my own good so that if I don't like it, I won't hold it against you.* "Can I offer a suggestion?" or "Can I ask you a question?" *So if I don't like what you say, I can't blame you because I agreed to listen.* "Okay, I'll just come out and say it," or "Let me get to the point," or "I'll cut to the chase." *Up to now you've been beating around the bush?* "I need to tell you something." *So, your need to say it outweighs whatever pain I may feel when I hear it.* "Don't take this the wrong way, but . . ." *You already seem pretty sure that I will take it the wrong way.* What all of these qualifiers have in common is the element of protection. The people using these qualifiers want to protect themselves from some predicted unpleasant reaction on the part of the person they're speaking to. They're attempting to lay some groundwork, smooth the path, shield themselves from harm. But their mind doesn't allow them to do this directly—that would be too scary. So it finds a way to make it sound like they're doing it for the other person's well-being. Pretty slick.

Perhaps you or someone you know is continually seeking truth, happiness, wisdom, enlightenment. So, isn't that what we're supposed to be doing? Aren't we here to find these things? Yes, yet how we go about it has a huge amount to do with whether we find what we're looking for. Seeking implies that what you're looking for is outside of you or your normal experience or that it's hidden or esoteric, or there must be some great effort expended to achieve it. While all of these things might be true, it's more than a little suspicious that they are exactly what your mind would want you to believe in order to keep the objective just out of reach.

When we seek, we may be doing it with the intention of demonstrating how hard we are working on ourselves, while our mind's goal is still to maintain the status quo. We get to appear highly motivated without actually doing anything that might require a change. And, if we are motivated to change, we are more likely to accept whatever comes along that is close to what we wanted. We may dumb down our ability to discriminate because our mind's goal is to be able to say that we either succeeded in finding what we were seeking or that it is unobtainable.

Often, we seek understanding, yet this too can be another way to control. We will say that we want to understand things, especially about our feelings, thoughts and behavior. When you notice something amiss, you might ask, "Why do I do that?" as if the whole of you was acting in this undesirable way. But the part that caused that behavior was your mind and it has again succeeded in hiding in the shadows by identifying itself with the entirety of who you are. How would the answer to that question be different if you asked instead, "How did my mind do that?" Additionally, our mind is saying, in effect, "Let me figure out what's going on so that I have a better chance of controlling it." If we improve our understanding of it, in this way, we become better able to deny or pretend or predict or prevent or fix or avoid all of those feared outcomes.

When we feel separate from ourselves, others or God, our mind has to find some way to deal with that pain. Early in our childhood, we were the center of the universe because we felt no boundary between ourselves and the environment. There was no need or ability to identify ourselves as separate because of the feeling of unity with everything. As we grew and that sense diminished, our mind needed to find a way to make up for what was perceived as missing. The most common way we make up for a sense of loss is to change what it means. Our mind, at that age, thought it was the only one that ever had to cope with this and, as the only one, it created for itself a position of specialness, of being different than everyone else. We didn't know that everyone goes through this apparent loss as a part of life experience. Being special is a comparison with others. Depending on the traits being compared, it can be higher or lower, better or worse but always different. In this case, different enough to be, somehow, outside the realm of fully human. And this difference, in of itself, allows our mind to create a feeling of being better or superior to others. A significant loss is compensated for with a significant gain.

Special usually takes one of two forms, victim or martyr. Our mind doesn't really care which and will often alternate between the two. What our mind needs is to be seen as different, both as an explanation for our feeling of separateness and as a justification for why that separateness continues. Special usually carries a story with it. It may be a story about a particular experience from childhood or it may be a story about a particularly difficult and long-lasting problem in our lives. Stories give us apparently good reasons as to why we haven't progressed beyond the limitations that we believe the experience has created. It could be as simple as, "Nobody understands me," which can be a fairly accurate perception, during adolescence, or it could be as complex as an unusually catastrophic, near-death, sole survivor experience. These experiences, we believe, have left us hurt, injured, broken or incomplete. Sometimes, special may be about a particular ability that we have, which seems to carry a cost in some other area of our life.

Aren't the superhero, mad genius, struggling artist, etc, usually alone?

There are several challenges in moving beyond these stories. One is that—your mind isn't going to like this—they're not true. Yes, your mind is convinced of their authenticity and accuracy but it's your mind that categorized and interpreted them to begin with. Your mind is going to filter, selectively recall, alter, judge, assign meanings, deny, pretend, etc., so that the story will suit your mind's purposes. Something happened, but, as is usually the case, other's recollection of the event will be different from yours. How do you know that yours is accurate and theirs is faulty? When it comes to recalling traumatic events from our past, our recollection will be much more of a reflection of our mind's agenda than of what actually occurred. And how long ago it was is not that important; your mind is doing this all the time. So if you had a particularly nasty break up with someone 10 years ago or 10 days ago, your mind will have done the same kind of magic act, to varying degrees, with both experiences.

It's quite possible to tell someone about an experience in your past with a minimum of mental static, but when you've listened to a number of these stories and remember how our minds work, you begin to feel how the stories have become permeated with our mind's interpretations. Our mind doesn't say, "Here's what actually happened but I'm choosing to remember and interpret it differently." We believe these stories because our mind recalls them that way. And, your mind can have a great time arguing about "the truth of what actually happened," which is pretty funny since, to our mind, truth is irrelevant when it comes to following its agenda of maintaining control.

Another difficulty with these stories is that they are self-reinforcing. Once your mind realizes that there's something to be gained in the retelling of these stories, it's going to do whatever it needs to get the most mileage out of them. Telling our stories to others frequently elicits interest, sympathy, advice or consolation. Reviewing them in our mind reinforces that sense of specialness that is like a soothing ointment on a wound. The wound is our perception of how we were hurt by the experience and the feeling of specialness acts as the balm. Each requires and maintains the other. This is another great example of how we create what we're trying to avoid. We don't want to feel separate so we come to believe we're special, and our specialness continually reminds us that we're different and separate.

We have all felt the righteous indignation of victimhood at one time or another. Just think of anything in your life that you perceived as unfair and, at the same time, felt powerless to change. A relationship that should have ended but didn't, a relationship you didn't want to end but did, a traffic ticket, not being selected for a promotion, an achievement or hard work not recognized by others, having a chronic illness, not getting something that someone else got, in fact, just about anytime we feel stuck or powerless, our mind will identify us as the victim. Our basic feeling of unfairness comes directly from being a little child in a world of big people who have all the power and who do what they believe is best for us, even when we think and feel otherwise. The feeling of unfairness often increases as we get older and usually is most pronounced in adolescence, when we think we're now old enough to make our own decisions but are still subject to the rules of others. That incredibly frustrating feeling of unfairness leads us right into victimhood. Once there, the only salve we can find for our wounds and pain is that sense of being special. Special restores some control to a situation that appears otherwise uncontrollable.

We have also felt the sacrificial empowerment of martyrdom at some point in our lives. Waiting to make sure everyone else get theirs, intentionally losing so someone else can win, not stating your desires and preferences, giving in instead of standing firm, taking the blame for something you didn't do, holding out hope long beyond any possibility of success, are all examples of how we generate a sense of martyrdom. The common thread in being a martyr is putting yourself last. Yet this tricky way of being last ends up putting yourself first! You get to be special through your sacrifice. Your mind will tell you that, no matter what else is going on, you're still a good person because of the way you take care of others. How do you feel about people you know who use this strategy? If you're not too fond of it, you may want to look at finding another way for yourself.

Using hypothetical situations is another way to avoid being present and responsible. Our mind wants to not only predict the future but to figure out all the possible variations of what might happen so it can control them too. Our mind may use predictions of undesirable outcomes as a way to inoculate us against fear; if we've imagined the worst and it doesn't happen, then our mind's prediction, though incorrect, will still feel like it had a useful purpose.

We use hypothetical situations to prepare ourselves for something that isn't even going to happen. Yes, your in-laws will probably show up for Thanksgiving and your boss may yell at you and your child may not want to go to college; however, each of these things will be a different event if you're actually present to experience it rather than letting your mind run the show. You can't be present and live out your mind's predictions at the same time. As much as it would like to, your mind can't predict the future. In the future, you will be different, other people will be different and the situation will be different. Predicting is not the same as planning.

Gifts are often used as a strategy, as well. Is a gift an exchange, a promissory note, a future obligation, a debt that can be called in? When used strategically, a gift can be any one or all of these things. Because most of us learned, growing up, that gift giving was an expected ritual, we, understandably, expect something in return. That something in return could be a gift given to us in a similar situation or it could, instead, be some anticipated future favor. So gifts often become a bribe or a statement about the future, saying, in effect, "I'll be expecting you to return this favor," or more directly, "You owe me." One of the more interesting variations of this is giving a gift as a way to make up for some perceived hurt. For example, if I hurt your feelings, I may buy you flowers or candy or something expensive as a way to, somehow, make up for my mistake. But if someone hurt you and they're taking responsibility for it, they would probably offer genuine recognition about how their actions affected you. Would you prefer gifts or a chance at greater intimacy?

Putting others on a pedestal is another common way of avoiding the responsibility of an equal relationship. Let's say I decide that you're better than me at expressing feelings. I've made a comparison and elevated you to a superior position over me, in this area. Now, any time it comes to expressing feelings, I've got an easy out. I've already decided that you're better than me, therefore, I'll never be as good as you, therefore, why bother? I'm doomed to fail. Doesn't make much sense, does it? And it doesn't allow for the possibility of new learning. Yet, that's exactly what our minds do whenever we elevate others above us. Now comes the even sneakier part. Do we really feel okay about being in a subordinate position, even if it's only about this one thing? No, we don't. First, because once we start putting people on a pedestal, we're going to do it in lots of areas. Second, if we make someone else special, we're going to have to find some way to maintain the balance and make ourselves special as well. Third, and perhaps, most humorous, is that once we've put someone up there, we start to resent that they're better than us! Yes, even though we put them on the pedestal, we still resent it. It's that amazing mind again, which can easily act as if what it's done was out of its control!

So, once we've got these people up on the pedestal, now we have to find a way to take them back down. And we don't do it the same way we put them up. No, now we're angry and resentful and we're going to pull them down in some nasty, hurtful way. It doesn't matter to us that they didn't know they were up there. How dare they think they're better than us? You don't even have to know someone to put them on a pedestal and then pull them down. Think about any typical social situation where the lives of public figures are being discussed. Listen and you will often hear admiration or envy of their wealth, status, accomplishments, etc., shortly followed by digs at their failure to maintain a relationship or marriage, sexual promiscuity, weight gains, drug problems, etc. Think about anyone in your life that you both like and resent and you're likely to find that you've put them on a pedestal.

Perhaps the grandest strategy of all is insisting that things be different than they are. This works so well because we can keep requiring others and circumstances to change while maintaining the illusion that we're simply waiting for the rest of the world to catch up with us. This is a very seductive strategy. It justifies what our mind believes, which is that, eventually, everyone else will see that we've been right all along. Right about our beliefs, right about our hurts, right about our stories, right about our resentments, etc.

This ultimate strategy of resistance brings up an important question. Is change more likely the result of others coming around to our way of thinking or is it something that we are doing differently? If it's us, what would make that change more probable? What could occur that would get us to stop banging our heads against the same wall believing that, if we just bang a little longer or a little harder, we'll be rewarded?

When we don't accept something we, in effect, deny its existence. That's exactly what our mind does whenever we refuse to accept things as they are. Our minds deny the existence of what is unacceptable by making it wrong. Of course, for something to be wrong, it would first need to exist, but our mind isn't easily confused by the facts. If that thing that I've made wrong doesn't exist, well then, I simply don't have to deal with it. I can go on, as I have been, without having to examine anything that I'm doing because I'm not the problem. You or it or they are the problem! When I don't accept that I make mistakes, I'm denying that I have the potential to make mistakes. If I don't accept that you have different opinions or desires or preferences than I do, I'm denying that you're different than me. And, believing that I don't make mistakes or that you and I are the same in all ways, will have some real undesirable implications for our relationship.

Perhaps change occurs after we first accept what is. And if I do accept what is? Not accept it begrudgingly but accept it, even welcome it all, as part of my humanness? Well, then I can stop beating myself up for my mistakes. Now I'm more willing to take risks. Now I'm more willing to be present because I'm not hiding. Now I don't need to predict the future or pretend to know. Now . . . everything can change.

There are many different strategies: Pick a time to talk about an emotional topic when you know the other person is tired or distracted. Exaggerate the importance of the topic. Use words like "always" and "never," even though you know they're not true. Come up with current or old complaints of your own in response to someone else's. Insist that this thing be resolved, now, or the relationship is at risk. Pull rank by using education, age, money, experience or other factors to communicate your superiority. Dominate by refusing to listen. Use labels like childish, insecure or overly sensitive to distract from the topic at hand. Tell the other person that you know the real reasons for their behavior or their real feelings. Predict a negative future to undermine the need to work things out. Use sarcasm. Say you don't remember what happened. Leave or threaten to leave. Give ultimatums. Reject compromise. Blame. Personalize what's going on to keep the other person on the defensive. Keep them off balance by changing your position. Use any combination of these. Make up your own. If there's a simple recipe for control, it would be to mix in a heap of judgment, a dollop of meaning, a handful of misperception and bake yourself up some tasty strategies.

You kind of have to admire how amazing our minds are in the variety of strategies and devices they develop to maintain control. And it's their very variety, which gives us so many opportunities to experience our minds at work. As we become less reactive, we can see and hear how our minds are constantly revealing themselves through their use of strategies, which become increasingly visible and transparent when we step back and look at what we're actually doing.

* * *

Q: *There are several people that have hurt me but when I try to forgive them, I don't feel any different, so what can I do?*

A: Forgiving someone while still making them wrong doesn't work. It's pretty clear that you can't drop a ball while still gripping it, yet that's what we often try to do, to let go while holding on. We want to forgive because we read it somewhere or a friend said we should or we even agree that it's a good idea. Wanting to forgive generally isn't enough if you've missed a couple of key steps.

Forgiveness usually requires that we first acknowledge that what happened is not the same as what we remember. Since it didn't happen the way we remember it, then it's possible that the people we believe wounded us didn't intend to do so. Maybe they were trying to help, even though we perceived it as hurtful. Maybe they were acting out of their own pain. Maybe they were still dealing with the experiences from their past which they, too, had not yet forgiven. Maybe our hurt has more to do with our desire to indirectly get back at them than the pain itself. Maybe they were having a really bad day.

One of the easy ways to know that your mind is maintaining its own version of the past is to look at the pain itself. When you recall the pain involved in the experience, does it really feel as hurtful as the level of pain described in your story about it? For example, on a scale of 1-10 with 10 being the worst, what level is the pain your mind says you experienced when this event occurred? Now, what level is the pain you actually feel, at this moment, regarding that event? If they're not the same, why not? Could it be that your mind is making more of this thing than it really is, by holding on to the past? If we can acknowledge that there was more to what happened than what our story tells and that our current discomfort is only based on our mind's story about the past, then lots of new, potentially healing, possibilities come into play.

Forgiveness also calls for us to fully accept our part in what happened as well. It may seem odd, yet, when we think we're having difficulty forgiving the other person, the real challenge is, often, forgiving ourselves. Why would we need to forgive ourselves? Well, simply, we were there. We were a participant. This is where our mind quickly reacts and we get stuck. "But, it wasn't my fault!" "I didn't do anything!" "I was only three years old!" "I yelled but he wouldn't stop!" "The car came out of nowhere!" Our mind will come up with a multitude of very rational sounding explanations as to why we have no responsibility for what happened. The predicament is this; if you weren't a participant, you were a victim, at least that's what your mind is going to insist. And, if you were a victim, your mind won't let you move on because victimhood and forgiveness can't exist at the same time. Oh, it may pretend to forgive, in which case, you become the martyr. But that's not any better, definitely not the same as forgiving.

Forgiveness doesn't mean that you forgive the other person from a place of being better than them or from greater understanding or having the generosity to grant them a pardon. Those are all simply more ways for our mind to maintain distance from what happened, to avoid looking at our part of the event. And what is our part in what happened? This is another place we get stuck. We think that having a part in what occurred means that we brought it on ourselves like a punishment for some unknown or imagined wrongdoing or that God was punishing us, which sounds a whole lot like being special! What if our part in what happens to us, the part we can own, is being present for our own learning and growth and being there for the learning and growth of others? It may seem at times, especially with the more difficult lessons, that learning is painful. It's not the learning that hurts as much as our resistance to going through the process of healing which causes the pain. And the resistance is our mind holding on for dear life.

Forgiveness is a form of letting go and releasing the hold the past has over you. Our mind wants us to believe that it's the people who hurt us and the experience itself that are preventing us from moving on when, actually, it's our mind's hold on the past that prevents our healing. We tend to think of forgiveness either as some beneficent act of kindness or some begrudging act of giving in. Forgiveness is more like saying goodbye. Goodbye to that part of your past that bound you, seemingly like a conjoined twin, and to those people you believed hurt you. Goodbye to that part of your mind that needed to hold on to the pain as a way of controlling others and maintaining your specialness.

Forgiveness cannot be forced or coerced. You can't simply do it because you should. In fact, you can't pretend at all because, with anything you "try to do," your mind gets into the act. Energy used exploring what you learned from the experience will move you closer to forgiveness than time spent replaying the pain and wrongness of it. Forgiveness occurs, spontaneously, when our humanness is no longer better or worse than the humanness of everyone involved.

PART 2

THE SIBLINGS
OF HEALING

6

LEARNING

Maybe I'm not too old for this stuff

Survival is imperative. Our mind, fearing that we will not survive, attempts to control that fear. In doing so, it continually pulls us into the emotional pains of the past or projects us into the mental anxieties of the future, thus obscuring our ability to be genuine and occupy the present. Our mind's habitual reactions hold no answers when we feel stuck or overwhelmed, yet physical, emotional and spiritual pain propel us to seek change. Healing starts as we become increasingly aware of our minds fear-based misperceptions and reactive control strategies. Healing continues as we tune in to the information available from other sources: our feelings, our body, other people, the environment and The Mind.

Healing calls for the recognition and fostering of self-trust. Self-trust deteriorates when we react to our mind's fear and need for control. Self-trust builds when we follow our gut, our heart and our intuition. Our mind will also want to control this; it will have to find the right way to heal. Well, there is no right way to heal and there is no wrong way. There are many paths and there is your path. Your process of change may be fast or slow, easy or difficult. Most likely, it will be all of these at different times.

Healing and learning are virtually the same. There may not be a lot of healing involved in learning a new recipe for scalloped potatoes, and you may not do a lot of learning because your mosquito bite heals. However, the healing of our deeper emotional, physical and spiritual ills is practically impossible without learning taking place. Learning to recognize our mind's protective mechanisms is a huge step toward healing the pain and fear that created those mechanisms in the first place.

One important source of healing information is our feelings. We aren't aware of the usefulness of our emotions because we take them for granted. And, thanks to our mind, we often have difficulty recognizing our feelings and frequently confuse thinking and feeling. Part of this is a learned emphasis on using our cognitive abilities at the expense of our capacity to feel. Part of it is due to our mind's habit of relying on thinking as a way to solve problems. And most of it is our mind's need to avoid feeling, which it finds unpredictable, fearful and difficult to control. Recognizing and acknowledging what we are feeling at any moment gives us access to one of the greatest forces of healing. What makes this such a powerful tool is that when we openly identify what we're feeling, we take a crucial step toward weakening our mind's power to control by hiding, altering or pretending that the feelings are not there. When we know what we're feeling, we're closer to our nature and to knowing how to be in different situations. When we feel who we are, as opposed to our mind's attempts at controlling what we do, we start to act out of self-trust rather than fear.

What happens when you're sad and pretend you're not? What happens when you're angry and deny it? What happens when you're happy and suppress it? What happens when you're afraid of your own fear? Well, perhaps you can see, by now, that when that happens, your mind is in control. And your mind will come up with perfectly good reasons for doing this. "He can't handle my tears." "She'll leave me if I really let her know how angry I am." "I can't be happy when everyone else is sad." "If I let go, I'm afraid I'll explode." So we pretend, deny and find ways to inhibit what we're feeling because it's too risky, too scary or not okay.

What happens to all of the pent-up energy associated with those unexpressed feelings? Does it just disappear like smoke in the wind? Unfortunately, no. When we don't express what we feel, at least to ourselves, we create doubt. Doubt starts to collect as a result of repeated instances of curbing and inhibiting what we feel. As children we are easily and completely expressive of our feelings. There is no reason not to be. As we grow and want to be loved, accepted and to fit in to our surroundings, we start to modify what, when and how much of our feelings are expressed. We get lots of messages about why we shouldn't express ourselves: "Mom has a headache," "Dad had a bad day at work," "That's not worth crying over," "Grow up," "Be a good boy or girl," "Take that tone out of your voice," "Don't upset me." Pretty soon, we start to wonder in what situations it's all right to express ourselves. Then we start to doubt if it's okay to express ourselves at all. Eventually, our mind succeeds in exerting control and we're no longer sure what we feel. And there is a further cost to not expressing ourselves. Like food for our body, air for our lungs and light for our nervous system, emotion is intended to pass through us, not be held onto. Years of unexpressed feelings build up and become like a toxin that will, eventually, harm us and others, as well.

Recall a time when you harshly unloaded on someone you weren't even that angry with or a time your tears expressed a sadness much greater than the pain of the moment. Some people seem to need the permission of alcohol or drugs to freely express themselves. Some people grit their teeth and clench their facial muscles rather than cry. What is unexpressed, with the original amount of associated energy, will, eventually, find a way out as a mutated form of the original. We don't get to feel things without sooner or later expressing them in some way.

When we hold on to feelings, we're telling others that it's not okay for them to fully express themselves either. You don't tell me anything I don't want to hear, and I won't tell you anything you're afraid of. Not a real good basis for an intimate relationship, is it? Rather than this arrangement increasing each other's comfort with the relationship, it accomplishes the opposite. Instead of giving each other the information needed to feel trusting of the other person and the relationship, this only serves to add to the doubt and fear.

Our body has a lot of information to give us, as well. What if our body isn't simply a device to help our brain survive, move us around from one place to another and reproduce? What if our body is a virtually untapped and unlimited source of information about our health, healing and ways to assist the healing of others? Once we start to turn off our mind's continual chatter, concern about right and wrong and the never-ending meanings that it assigns to everything, we can begin, again, as we did in our infancy, to learn what our body has to tell us.

Our body serves as an ever-present source of healing information. Take food, as an example. Do you sometimes have difficulty knowing when you're hungry? Do you frequently eat simply based on the time of day or eat to the point of feeling overly full? Do you have difficulty deciding what to eat? Have you wondered why there's a lot more obesity in developed countries? Do any of the other creatures on this planet, except, perhaps, domesticated animals and pets, seem to ignore their body's messages in this way?

Most of us grew up eating at certain times of the day, eating quantities and eating types of foods that were determined by others. How does someone else know when we're hungry, how much we want to eat and what we want to eat? They don't. But being dependent on them and wanting to please, we usually went along and, like good boys and girls, ate everything on our plate. So, it's not too surprising that, as adults, we're out of touch with our body's need for food. We often don't know when we're hungry because we eat so frequently. We don't know how much our body needs to feel satisfied because we habitually eat beyond the point of satiation. We've lost touch with the ability to feel what foods our body needs because we usually eat what's in front of us, what's quick and what's convenient. This is one of the reasons that diets often don't work in the long run; it's still someone else's idea of what or how often or how much you should eat.

What would it take to get reacquainted with your body's messages about food? It requires recognizing that our mind often uses food as a form of emotional nourishment. To our mind, eating three meals a day and snacks, like we did as children, or eating that special comfort food may be a way we can still feel loved. Learning to express what you feel reduces the need to use food to numb yourself. It calls for delaying eating until you start to feel what might be hunger. When you start to feel hunger, you will also begin to feel what your body is hungry for, which may be different than what is readily available.

When eating is based on hunger, you also learn to feel the end of hunger, which goes along with eating slow enough to feel that point of satiation and has little to do with how much food is in front of you. At this point, you may be saying to yourself that this is going to be too much work or not possible with your busy schedule or not worth the effort. This isn't simply about the food we eat. Our body is constantly sending us messages about its need for water, nutrients, air, light, temperature, touch, movement, activity, etc. If we numb ourselves in any area, we numb our ability to feel in other areas as well. If we aren't able to feel what our body wants to keep it healthy, is it surprising that we have difficulty feeling what we want in other areas of our lives? Our mind, so wrapped up in its need for control, is quite willing to sacrifice our body's health for its agenda. Are you?

Sometimes, it seems like we've entered a foreign country where the inhabitants do really strange things. We often find it much easier to recognize the oddities in other people's thinking and behavior while ours remains a mystery to us. We often don't realize how counterproductive our thoughts and behavior are until sometime afterwards. We may feel uncomfortable but still go ahead and finish what we're saying or doing even though we strongly suspect we're going to regret it later.

The people in our world can offer a wealth of information about our healing. Sometimes it's direct, as when you read a book, like this one, or take a workshop or study with a teacher. More often though, it's indirect, such as when you're talking with a friend or stranger and they say something which allows you to see yourself in a different way. And, frequently, if your mind is quiet, you can learn a vast amount by simply watching and listening to others. That's the way that we started all of this learning, as infants and children. We watched and listened and copied and experimented and kept what we liked and discarded the rest.

In a way, our use of the term "adult" is unfortunate because, for most of us, it says that we've arrived at the place we always thought we'd get to as children. Adults are big and make their own decisions and they can do whatever they want. Well, that's what we believed, anyway. Is that the way it turned out? Yes, we're bigger now, but how many adults do you know that aren't still stuck in their meanings, judgments, strategies, beliefs, fears, doubts, etc.? How many of us grew up to be the adults we thought we would be? There's nothing wrong with this and it doesn't mean anything about you. It is a clue that we're all in the same boat. We all have a lot of learning to do. People are like ice cream. We all have the same basic ingredients, and come in a variety of flavors. Despite what our mind tells us, based on its need for control, we all face similar challenges and also have the facility to support and enhance each other's learning.

When we stop or at least reduce the mental noise, we get to see, hear and feel what's going on from a different perspective—from The Mind. Denial, pretense, avoidance, fear, strategies, labels, comparisons, beliefs, stories, etc., all start to become visible to us. At first, we still can't easily see them in ourselves and it's a lot easier to see them in others. That's okay. We're learning, so it's going to take time and repeated experiences and we're going to make many mistakes, all of which is necessary for learning and, when our mind is napping, doesn't mean anything.

Learning is what we start to do even before we're born and we continue through death. It almost never occurs to us to say, "Wait a second, all I'm doing right now, despite the apparent pain and drama and mental stuff, is learning." Were we to remember that learning is taking place, all the time, it would give us a calmer place from which to experience what's occurring without all the meanings and judgments and strategies. Further, when we're learning, it helps us to see that there is no right or wrong or good or bad in the situation. We may like it or not, we may want to repeat it or not, we may want to share it or not, and all of that is separate from anything that our mind will try to make of it. Imagine how much easier and, probably, faster your healing will be when you start to bring to each experience the predisposition of learning.

Learning, for a child, means making many, many, many, what adults call, mistakes. Infants don't have the slightest idea of what a mistake is. Kids drop things, spit up, pee and poop all the time, bump into things, knock stuff over, fall, trip, fall some more, all without an iota of self-criticism or doubt about their value or capacity to learn. They only attach a meaning to their behaviors when we start to communicate it to them as they begin to look and listen for our responses. As babies, we could spend the whole day fearlessly, happily, playfully learning how to crawl, sit, stand, walk, eat, smile, laugh, etc., because our mind had no need to control those functions. As adults, we often have a very difficult time learning because now we have a mind telling us we're doing it wrong! After years of listening to our minds telling us that we'll never get it right, it's not too hard to see that the very process of learning brings up doubt and dread and "Do I have to?" Intellectually, we know that learning is a process of trial and error, yet our minds will insist that, even when we're learning, we have to get it right the first time!

Healing, when it happens, is not filtered through our mind. Healing circumvents our mind and enters the body in other ways, at other levels. But when it comes to learning what we need, in order to change and grow, our minds have a whole slew of fears, doubts and beliefs and with all that weight we're carrying around, it's not hard to see how healing usually takes a lot of time.

Change is a process of letting go of what no longer serves us, such as the strategies, filters and beliefs that we developed as children. We still carry them, though, like excess baggage, though we often no longer feel how they weigh us down due to our mind's ability to hide and the habits we've developed. When you do feel bogged down by your life, what you're actually experiencing is your mind's hold on the meanings it has assigned to past experiences. Your mind will tell you it's your job, money, relationship, kids, health, etc., but most of that is your mind's projection of a fearful future based on a painful past and its need to control.

We usually think of learning as a process of collecting, building and increasing the contents of our knowledge. Actually, the most critical learning we do is a process of exclusion. As babies, we learned to use our bodies by making many different movements. We only kept the ones that worked and discarded or excluded the rest because they were not congruent or pleasurable with what we were learning at the time. A baby, learning to grasp a ball, will, at first, not succeed because the neurological wiring for the task is not in place. It will bump into the ball, use the back of its hand or mouth, use some fingers and not others, make other unrelated body movements, sounds, facial expressions, etc. In other words, it will explore a large variety of possible actions to grasp the ball. Only those movements that feel successful will be kept and repeated and everything else will be let go.

This is the same kind of learning essential for healing. Healing is learning to not do or not repeat something that doesn't achieve the desired results. Why would we hold onto and repeat behaviors that don't achieve the desired results? For the same reasons our mind tells us that pleasing the other person is more important than our own success: habit, doubt, fear, control.

As adults, we often fail to distinguish advantageous movement from disadvantageous movement. We learned as babies what helps accomplish the task versus what interferes with the task, but as adults we usually have conflicting imperatives. We want to be intimate and not get hurt. We want to take a risk and stay safe. We want to grow and not let go of the past. So, our mind leads us to do funny things. We say "Yes" with our mouth while our body is saying "No." We open our hands while protecting our hearts. Our heads move forward while our feet step backward. We reach out with our arms while our pelvis backs away.

Much thought and research has gone into figuring out how we are different from animals. More recently, discoveries have been made about how much of our genetics are the same as other primates and how, in many ways they are like us. Perhaps even greater learning lies in exploring how we are like them, not just primates but the entire living world. Babies and animals eat when they're hungry and sleep when they're tired. Adult humans eat and sleep by the clock. Babies and animals, when given choices, seem to eat according to their body's nutritional needs, at the time. Adult humans eat what's convenient, cheap or quick. Animals have built in patterns for mating and child rearing, according to their species. Humans have a variety of options for mating and child rearing and some of the possibilities work some of the time. There are no right and wrong answers here. While animals are not human, humans are animals. We're animals with brains that have enlarged capacities for learning, thought, emotion, intuition, connection, imagination, etc. If we distance ourselves from the rest of the living world, we miss out on the chance to learn valuable information about both who we are and who we can be.

It may seem as if there are different kinds of healing and, therefore, different things we need to learn and do for each one. Physical healing is primarily addressing an injury, disease or condition in our body. Emotional healing pays attention to the fear and pain that we experience. Spiritual healing works on our doubts and beliefs about our belonging and life purpose. While the primary focus of each one may be different, there is often a large overlap, such that work in one area leads to healing in another. Our mind will try to control the process by telling us that they are separate and different and that we need to do it right in order to heal.

As you might expect, when our mind does change, it does so in a very controlled way. When you grasp, for example, that what you recall about past events did not happen exactly the way you remember it, your mind may say, in effect, "I knew that" or "Okay, no big deal." Your mind incorporates the changes and then continues about its agenda as if nothing happened. It can't question or wonder how it was operating on faulty or incomplete information all this time—otherwise it might begin to question all of its operations.

Our mind can also get stuck on the specific "lesson" we think we're supposed to be learning. Once we get the idea that learning is ever-present our mind often takes over to figure it out. Say you started out talking to your adolescent son about cleaning his room and it somehow turned into a shouting match ending with anger and hurt on both sides. What's the lesson? That you shouldn't talk about this subject? That you addressed it at an inopportune time? That you expect too much? That he doesn't understand what you want? That he is just a slob? That it's really about the expectations placed on you as a child? You may well not know, at the time, what the lesson is. What you can be reasonably sure of, though, is that, if your mind is involved, it will try to arrive at an answer that will allow some rapid resolution in order to avoid lingering discomfort. If you can circumvent your mind's pressure to quickly figure it out, the real learning will, eventually, be revealed.

* * *

Q: *What can I do to learn and heal more effectively?*

A: Assessing differences is how we learn. It's the way our nervous system is designed. Our brain is continually assessing, measuring and evaluating. If we did not do this automatically, babies would never learn how to move, walk, talk and all of the many other amazing capacities we have. Novelty feeds our curiosity and stimulates our attentiveness. Repetition puts our brains to sleep and allows our mind to take over. You cannot coerce learning. When you do, your mind may go along while your intuition rebels. Coercing yourself to learn is like trying to lead a horse by its tail.

Healing is like raising your own kid. How would you want to learn? What would you want your teacher to do to support you? There is no right or best way to learn, though there may be a better way for you, at a particular time, regarding a particular matter. And there are some ways to make it easier.

Look for the pattern. This is especially applicable to any areas in which you seem to repeatedly experience less than desirable results. Take relationships, as an example. How do you begin? How do you feel as you begin? How do you meet? Who initiates? How are decisions made? How direct are you in stating your desires and preferences? What do you fear? How does the relationship progress? How does it end? There are many possible questions like this. The point is to ask questions which provide useful information, rather than those designed to figure out who's right, who's wrong or who's at fault. You can then honestly look, in detail, at what has happened in the past. You may like the pattern, but, if not, figure out or get some help from others to figure out what the pattern is and what could be done differently.

Explore and play. We get so busy doing things that we forget how we originally learned. Babies don't do tasks, chores, projects or activities. They explore and play. They learn through playful interaction with the world. As adults, we tend to be either serious or we take time off from being serious, which is not the same as play. Exploration and play involves using a beginner's mind, being in The Mind, being free from any need to accomplish or perform. We may think that performance anxiety is something that only musicians and athletes experience. Most of us have it most of the time.

Experience what is, rather than your judgments. As soon as you notice you've made a judgment about anything or assigned a meaning to it, about you or others, you're out of the experience and into your mind. Find a way to give yourself a signal, which becomes pretty automatic, each time judgment and meaning come up. When they do, thank your mind and come back to the experience. It may take many, many repetitions of this before your mind finally shuts up. Stay with it and then determine for yourself if you liked the experience better with your mind quiet or active.

Improve what you already do well, rather than trying to fix problems. We tend to get preoccupied and highly charged about whatever we've identified as the problems of our lives, which have to be fixed in order for us to feel okay. What if we let all that go and focused instead on what we're already good at? Our mind, of course, will say this makes no sense. Why waste time on something that doesn't need to be fixed? When we do something we already feel good about, we're more likely to do it with a sense of freedom and play, compared to the seriousness and drama we bring to something we've identified as a problem. When we do something we already feel good about, we're using our energy in a way that enhances our self-trust, rather than diminishing it. And, often, when fully engaged in what we do well, we gain previously hidden awareness about the imagined problem, which allows us to come up with a different and more successful approach.

Recognize and accept what is, before looking to change. What we think we need to fix and change is usually not that well understood by us because our mind is controlling it. What we call the problem is, frequently, our mind's attempt to mask our fear by getting busy doing something. We're not aware of the judgments and meanings and ways that we've misperceived; all we know is that we've got to fix it. When our energy is focused on doing, we have very little left for recognizing what we've missed and we're unable to accept what is. Our mind believes that accepting what is means that we give up on fixing it and, therefore, it's un-fixable. In this case, our mind is correct, though not for the reasons it thinks. When we accept what is, we do give up on fixing it, because there's nothing to be fixed. When we accept what is, all of our energy is now available to look at new possibilities.

Keep asking, "What would be the easy way?" We are so habituated to struggle that we accept it as normal. When we accomplish something without a lot of effort, we may even believe we must have done it wrong. Learning is not intended to be a struggle. If it were, babies would give up and few would learn to walk and talk. When we are wrestling with something we're trying to learn, it's not the thing itself that's causing the difficulty, it's our mind's predetermined objections that we're struggling with, its beliefs about what should and shouldn't be, that are getting in the way. When we stop and ask ourselves and others if there's some less effortful way to do it, we start to let go of our mind's insistence on doing it right and open up to the possibility that there may be one or more different and easier ways of being. Your mind may be saying, "Sure I can be lazy and cut corners," but it confuses work and effort. Work is the amount of energy it takes to complete the task. We use effort and struggle when we believe we're not good enough.

Rest when you need to, even in the middle of something. We have this value or belief that says you should stick with what you're doing, until it's done. We're also used to having someone else give us permission to stop and take a break. It's quite difficult to both do and pay attention at the same time. Taking breaks or rests, even if it's not in sync with what everyone else is doing, reinforces your responsibility to give yourself permission, breaks up the routine, is respectful of your pace and, most importantly, gives you a chance to reflect. Nonstop doing is okay when there's a routine and practiced task to be accomplished. It's just not very helpful when it comes to learning new skills.

Go slow. We live much of our lives as if they are a race and then are often uncomfortable when we have nothing that needs to be done. We get habituated to a certain amount of activity and pace and then often have difficulty resting when rest is truly needed. We tend to want to move quickly in learning situations as well. But how do you move quickly if you don't know what you're doing? And if you're learning, then you're not going to know what comes next. Your mind will want to know and predict and will often fake it in the hope of avoiding what it fears. Going slow helps you to pay attention to the details, and that tends to push the snooze button on your mind's alarm system.

Trust what you feel and distrust what you think. Our minds have us so reliant on them that we often forget how useful our feelings are as a guide to our own process. We think it's our feelings that get us in trouble, but, of course, that's what our minds want us to believe. Getting reacquainted with your emotions may be as simple as frequently asking yourself, throughout the day, how you're feeling. Sometimes the answer will be that you don't know. Sometimes it will be a sensation like cold or hunger or tired or tight. Sometimes it will be a feeling like anxious or relieved or happy or upset. Whatever the feeling is, find the place in your body that is connected with it. Feelings are based in the body. Getting comfortable with your body, in this way, helps you to regain this vital source of information that's been dulled or forgotten. Besides the things we usually identify as feelings, let intuition become as real and comfortable for you as your favorite pair of shoes.

Find a healing path that works for you. Healing that seems to work best for most people, in the long run, usually doesn't exclude anything that's part of the human experience. It incorporates mind, emotion, body, spirit and other levels of consciousness. And, it places more value on the student's own learning process and discoveries than simply following or imitating the teacher's directions. Be willing to experiment and remember that teachers do not have to be perfect for you to learn a great deal from them. Most importantly, trust your intuition.

Do what feels important in the moment. Often, especially in a group situation, where we have labeled our role as student and another's role as teacher, we believe that we must follow the teacher's directions, exactly, in order to learn what we're supposed to. Most of this is our mind seeking approval and wanting to fit in. At any time, however, an impulse can arise to do something different from the rest of the group. Call it intuition or curiosity or a wild hair; the explanation isn't as important as giving yourself permission to follow it and see where it leads. Becoming our own teachers and exploring for ourselves is the way we learned as babies and is still the most reliable way to make a lasting change. Following the person in front of us did not lead to the vast majority of our great discoveries. How we hold ourselves back from this is the fear that we'll be missing out on what we came to learn or that we'll be judged as disruptive or different. Is our mind good at control, or what?

Be present. Occupying your body, in other words, continually feeling who you are, is a great way to be present. Imagine your body trying to operate, now, on old data about your heart rhythm, pulse rate, respiration, hormone levels, brain waves, etc. Or, imagine your body trying to predict how it will function tomorrow with no idea whether it will be dealing with a call from a childhood friend or an auto accident. Our mind does this time travel stuff all the time, so it's fortunate that our body has primary responsibility for keeping us alive. When we're present, we occupy The Mind, and all the habitual judgments and meanings don't exist. We then become unencumbered by everything that we believed we were, are free to learn what's true for us now, and are fully capable of dealing with whatever comes tomorrow.

Catch your mind in the act. When we recognize that our mind is in control we make the fundamental step toward change. Let's say I come home from work and, while helping my son with his homework, I make a judgment about his apparent disinterest or short attention span. Later I realize that I was actually angry about an earlier unpleasant interaction with someone at work and it had nothing to do with my child. The next step is to identify what led me to do this, to recognize my mind in operation, and to make the connection between my behavior and the fear or other feelings that led to that behavior. Every time we catch our mind in the act, even hours, weeks or years later, we shrink its power to control and are halfway toward a new possibility. The second half is our decision to make a change.

7

PERMISSION

I didn't fix it and nobody died?

We sometimes find ourselves in situations or conversations feeling lost, confused, frustrated, angry, etc. It's easy for this to happen when our mind is full of the judgments, meanings, perceptions and beliefs through which it attempts to control the world. It's especially likely when we are heavily invested in particular relationships such as with God, our family of origin, significant others, friends or work. We can be aware that our mind is operating at full speed, yet we often don't give ourselves permission to simply stop and get off that express train that we never even intended to board. Giving yourself permission is like giving yourself a breather, a step back for a larger or broader perspective, a moment to reflect without having to act. We feel the pressure to respond because we believe we must give quick answers in order to be loved. The child wants to know so it can give the right answer while the adult can take the time to listen, learn and use a beginner's mind.

Identifying the emotional charge such as confusion, anger, self-righteousness, etc., is the red flag that tells you it's time to take a break from the conversation, go for a walk or hang up the phone. Without permission, the chances of clearly feeling, seeing and hearing what is going on, both within and outside of you, are greatly reduced. It really is okay to take a break; it's not a life or death situation, only your mind telling you so. You can always come back later and continue. Permission is like a wise person behind you who stops the action and says, "This is a good time to stop, take a break and look inside to feel what's going on." It's very hard to feel, see or hear clearly when the scared child, your mind, is in charge of the action. When you're ready, whether it's moments or months later, you can come back to the point when you gave yourself permission to stop and, then, continue. It may feel like it's really serious or it's critical that it be resolved immediately, but that's your mind talking.

Recognizing your red flag is a key to changing the dynamic of the interaction. Like many things that we wish and search for, the red flag is already there. It's that feeling of wanting to strangle the other person. It's that desire to scream out of frustration. It's wanting to slam the phone down. It's right in front of us, waving madly and we don't recognize the signs that any outside observer would immediately see. We're so wrapped up in being right, making it about us, finding a solution, trying to help, needing to be loved, etc. that we readily lose ourselves in our mind's programming

Permission is intimately related to self-trust and choice. The feeling that we are stuck, which is a lack of permission to look for, identify or choose another option, is perhaps one of the most subtly destructive feelings there is. Remember, we're not feeling stuck because of actual limits on what we can do. We're feeling stuck because we misperceive that there are no other options. Feeling that you have a choice is much more important than the variety of choices themselves or even which option you end up choosing. Much of our stuckness comes from failing to realize that at a certain point in our development, we started to give ourselves permission. It may have started by saying, "No" or rebelling in other ways. But because it started out as a reaction to another person, we don't recognize it as permission. When that other person is no longer around, we find it difficult to do it for ourselves. We're caught in the belief that permission is something given to us by someone else. We'll keep waiting for it until we realize that we can give it to ourselves.

Children need permission to do things that might threaten their safety. Adults don't need anyone's permission but act like they do and, therefore, get stuck because they don't see the choices that are already available. You have a choice whether you get out of bed in the morning. You have a choice whether or not you go to work. You have a choice whether you live or die. Your mind will not want to see that these are real choices. It says, "I don't have a choice." "I have to take care of my family." "I must work." Yet, this is where permission starts. If we don't recognize that each perceived obligation is actually a choice that we habitually ignore, then the range of our choices gets smaller and smaller over time and is reflected as contraction in our bodies, our emotions and in many other areas of life. This is not to say that you shouldn't work or support the people you love, rather, it points out how we frequently get stuck in the ways we generalize. Habit is an unrecognized choice that eventually, with enough repetitions, convinces you there is no choice. In much the same way that, if we don't welcome responsibility, we will feel like victims, if we don't choose, every day, and give ourselves permission, we will feel trapped with no way out.

In the learning process, our brain and mind function primarily as mechanisms of inhibition. If our mind were to be located in a specific area of the brain, it seems likely that it would reside in our frontal lobe which develops last, both from an evolutionary perspective and chronologically in our development. Our frontal lobe is where we seem to do most of our higher level thinking. One of the ways we know this is that when the frontal lobe is damaged by disease or injury, a common behavior change is disinhibition; what used to be held back, no longer is. People with frontal lobe injury may freely curse, shed their clothes, and behave in a very sexualized manner. We also know this from watching infants learn. When you watch a young child experimenting with movement, say, learning to stand, they don't actually learn what to do. Rather they learn what not to do. Every time they make a movement, which doesn't feel good or doesn't get the desired results, they try something different. Ultimately, they keep the movements that work and inhibit the ones that don't. This is the ideal state, where their learning is not interfered with by any preexisting limitation and takes place in an atmosphere of play and support. They have full and complete permission, until we start to place limits on them; some to maintain safety, some out of our need for control.

Just as inhibition of extraneous movement is the primary way our brain develops our neuromuscular system, inhibition of feeling is the primary way our mind develops control. And just as the messages that our brain inhibits would otherwise interfere with the desired movement, the feelings that our mind inhibits would otherwise prevent its successful control. In other words, recognizing and expressing what you feel, at least to yourself, lessens your mind's control. In this way, the common phrase that we use to say that someone's behavior or actions are unacceptable or scary, takes on a wholly new and very different meaning. What *will* it take for you to finally and thankfully be "out of control?"

We talk about "human nature" and "natural behavior" as if we can easily distinguish between genetics and learning, as if we can clearly identify what causes us to act the way we do. Perhaps one day we will all agree on exactly what we're born with versus what we learn. What is more relevant to healing, though, is how aware we can be of our mind's activities and how we react or not to our minds stories. As we develop, our mind takes over the role of the one who is withholding permission: to stop, to start, to come, to go, to change the rules, to change at all.

After a certain point in our development, usually around age 4, we become almost exclusively dependent on our minds and on language for our learning. We stop distinguishing between feelings and thoughts and the words we use to describe them. Indeed, it becomes almost impossible for us to have thoughts and feelings without putting them into words, even if we're only talking to ourselves. Because our experiences become virtually inseparable from the words we use to describe them, we tend to habitually use the same words to talk about the things we're struggling with. Using the same words to talk, think or feel about any particular experience activates the same habitual associations of thought, feeling and behavior. Our mind avoids using different words because that might lead to thinking or feeling or perceiving things differently than the way in which it maintains control. So, changing how we feel about our experiences and who we are in relation to them, is also supported by an associated change in the words used to describe those experiences and feelings.

We tend to use global, all-encompassing words like always, never, have to, must, should, can't, etc., when we're talking about unpleasant experiences from the past, the way they impact us now and the obligations which we resent. Just as our brain works by carefully distinguishing small differences in color, light, heat, pressure, etc., our mind starts to lose some of its control when we begin to distinguish differences in feelings. There really is a huge difference between "I always pick the wrong people to date!" and "Something about my choices for romantic partners isn't working out and I'd like to find out what that is." The first statement makes a judgment and implies a black and white condition with little if any possibility for change. The second statement identifies an unsatisfactory situation, recognition of a desire for a different choice and the possibility of change. This is more than simply semantics. Using different words, especially those that are not heavily laden with judgment, meaning, misperception and strategy, circumvents our mind's habitual control mechanisms and increases the likelihood of a different outcome.

* * *

Q: *How do I give myself more permission, when I don't even know that I'm holding myself back from doing so?*

A: Lack of permission is, mostly, a reflection of our unwillingness to accept what is. Acceptance is an essential kind of permission. It's permission to stop fighting against the world, against God, against others and against ourselves. We invest so much time and energy trying to change what is, trying to prove we're right, that we often fail to realize what we're actually doing. Permission first requires recognition and acceptance of whatever's going on right now in order to then identify what we'd like to be different.

Let's say you're in a relationship that is just the way you want it, in most ways, and there are a few things you'd like to be different. What are the options? You can keep expecting the other person to read your mind and continue to be unhappy when he/she doesn't. You can say to yourself that it's better not to rock the boat and just be happy with what you have. You can use any one of a number of strategies to try and get the other person to change. None of these are likely to work very well, if at all. It's not just that they're ineffective means of expressing your desires; they won't work because you probably haven't taken the first step, which is to truly accept what is. Instead, you're denying your feelings or pretending they don't matter because your afraid of what might happen if you directly expressed them. Acceptance includes accepting what feels unacceptable. This is how our mind works. It limits our permission to try something different by judging our desires and through the fear of losing what we already have.

One of the big things we have in our favor, though unfortunately we often forget it, is that the other person usually has similar fears. So when one of you is courageous enough to take the risk of saying how you feel, it's usually a relief to the other person because now he/she has increased permission as well. We all would like something to be different in our lives but we've gotten so many silly messages like, "You can't have your cake and eat it too," that we've fallen into the trap of believing our mind's self-imposed limitations.

Of course, how you express your desire has a lot to do with how successful the outcome is. Blame, victimhood, martyrdom, judgment, etc. tend not to put others at ease or increase their receptiveness to what we have to say. We often hold on to our unspoken desires for so long that, when they do come out, they are expressed with a charge that is much greater than the situation calls for. Permission, in the form of accepting what is, allows us to express ourselves in a much more timely, clear and direct way.

Whenever we identify the feeling that goes along with not expressing ourselves, there's a good chance that permission is being withheld. Sometimes you may choose to delay expressing what you feel or to not express it at all. However, if you don't clearly identify the feeling and express it, at least, to yourself, you continue to reinforce your mind's control. It could be as simple as "Oh, I'm feeling sad," or "Oh, yeah, that's anger." Giving yourself permission to recognize and accept what is, creates a new foundation for change. Will you get what you want, just because you've expressed it and even expressed it in the best way for the other person to hear it? Not necessarily, but getting it is not really the point of saying what you want or how you feel. Permission is it's own reinforcement. The more we do it, the more often we're successful. More permission leads to more learning, more self-trust and more pleasure with our lives and choices. Giving ourselves permission is essential to becoming our own supportive and loving brothers or sisters. When we do this, those parts that have been cut off or suppressed for many years, now have a chance to surface, be expressed and be seen.

8

ACCEPTANCE

If you're not responsible then... I am!

The choice to be born, to incarnate, to come to Earth in physical form, is a statement of our desire to heal, grow and evolve. Yet, we commonly spend much of our time either pretending we don't want to be here or denying that this was our choice. But we are here. The choice has already been made. One of our often-used disclaimers is, "I didn't ask to be born!" The implication being, therefore, "I'm not responsible for my life or anything else." Our mind will deny that we are responsible for anything we do while at the same time maintaining that others are responsible not only for their lives but for ours. Pretty funny.

Denying responsibility for incarnation is not only a good foundation for victimhood, it also postpones healing. Accepting responsibility for being here is the foundation for adulthood. When we do this, it becomes much more difficult to blame others, whether that pain is due to early trauma, accident, illness, a bad day at work, troubled relationship or whatever. And, when we accept this responsibility it becomes much easier to effectively alter our life to move it in the direction of life purpose. In other words, we start to struggle a lot less.

The ramifications of choosing to be here include living in a physical body, birth, death, feeling, gender, gravity, affecting others and being affected by others. All of these factors make life challenging while, at the same time, creating continuous opportunities for learning. We often find ourselves caught in situations that are painful and difficult and we don't understand how we got there or how to move through them. Remembering we chose to be here is of huge value in taking responsibility and doing what needs to be done. Accepting responsibility for that choice is also the foundation for being present. When you're present, your mind is no longer running the show and The Mind becomes available.

"Doesn't she see . . .?" "Why can't he . . .?" How come those idiots don't know . . .?" "When will I finally . . .?" Have you heard yourself or others asking these kinds of questions? They're not really questions, of course. They're the judgments we make when we can't accept how things are. Not accepting what is, keeps our mind perpetually busy, forever occupied with figuring out how to change reality.

We often confuse what happened to us with how we feel about it. This can make life difficult in a number of ways. It's easy to see how sugar, eggs, flour, etc., are the separate ingredients of the cake before its baked, in other words, before the cake exists. But, suppose you want to look at the ingredients afterwards so you can examine them in more detail. How do you separate out just the flour from the cake, after it's baked? Our experiences are like that. We absorb whole events and forget that they had multiple separate components. So, later, when we taste those emotional or mental components, by themselves, our mind often generalizes to the whole experience. This can be seen more easily in any traumatic event such as child abuse, the unexpected death of a loved one, etc. There are all of the emotions, beliefs and misperceptions about the other person and then there are all of those pieces, as well, about the traumatic event itself. This multiplicity of components is present in anything that happens, though perhaps with lesser intensity. When we remember an experience, all of the emotional and cognitive connections that go along with it are also there and how we feel about it becomes very difficult to separate from what happened. This is fine with our mind because it's simple and controllable.

Acceptance is easier when we are able to differentiate what happened from how we feel about it. Otherwise, we will continue to distance ourselves from what happened as a way of avoiding the unpleasant feelings. This becomes a huge impediment to acceptance because we think that accepting what happened means we must, at the same time, let go of all of the connected grief, loss, anger, hurt, disappointment, etc. Additionally, our mind insists on its position of being the victim in what happened and we hold onto these feelings as our justification for that position. As the process of separating the event from the feelings continues, the feelings, too, come to be accepted because they're no longer stuck in the past with the experience. They can then be fully felt and released.

It is the absence of meaning, judgment, control, misperception and strategies that allows us to feel our preexisting state of connection and happiness. Acceptance of what is cancels out all of that mental stuff, which is constantly flooding us with messages that either we're not good enough, the other person is not okay, the situation is not right or whatever problem our mind has identified at that moment. Acceptance allows us to see that the problem is not a problem; it's only whatever our mind has chosen to focus on. Without acceptance, we're limited to moving from one problem to the next in an endless cycle.

We sometimes get confused between questioning what we're doing and being in doubt. When you're questioning, your desire is to understand. When you're in doubt, your mind is looking for the wrongness in what you or someone else is doing. Doubt colors our feelings. When we don't feel good about ourselves, doubt is present; doubt about our wholeness, our connectedness, our ability to support ourselves, our ability to love and be loved, in short, doubt about our life purpose.

We tend to approach situations with a preexisting position about them. We already have an idea about the likely outcome, how things should be, how we should behave and feel and think. This positionality strongly influences the outcome. It doesn't guarantee what will happen, even our minds aren't that powerful, but it does tend to push things in a particular direction. Our mind's positionality is like a strong bias for a particular result because, even when we say we want something different, we're more comfortable with what we know. Habit, judgment, meaning, strategies and pain are what our minds know, and we will often take those in place of something different because after so many years, they have become like a well-worn suit of clothes. Judgment is the glue that holds the habits of our mind in place. Acceptance is the solvent that allows us to move out of our programmed positionality and find new relationships to the world.

Acceptance includes accepting responsibility. Pushing away responsibility for how our lives are, at any moment, prevents us from accepting what is. We often have a lot of trouble with this one because our mind keeps telling us that other people are more responsible for our lives than we are. After all, we had so little power to change things when we were babies. We were born into a situation that was already in place and for so many years we had to do what we were told. Our minds love this argument because it sounds so believable. It's seductive because it has the ring of truth and it's an experience that everyone has shared. However, it's thin soup. It doesn't really nourish you and it also doesn't allow you to move forward. As long as you're holding on to that one, true healing is going to be very limited.

Perhaps there's a way to allow for the strong influence of others in our lives while, at the same time, taking responsibility for ourselves. How about if you're 50% responsible for what happens when there are other people involved? The remaining 50% is their responsibility. And, even if there are three or more people involved, each one is still 50% responsible. Otherwise, your mind will use the math as a convenient way out, an excuse for avoiding ownership. And yes, this includes when you were a baby—our mind really hates that one. Now, here's the easier part. You're 100% responsible for how you feel about what happens. After all, no one, except your mind, is telling you how to feel about things. Even if you still want to deny your responsibility for what happens, it's pretty hard to deny that your feelings about it are your own. While it's true that much of our feelings are learned from others, whether or not we still feel that way is wholly up to us. Just taking full responsibility for how you feel pushes you in the direction of change because, if you don't like the feeling, you'll be inclined to alter the situation where it occurs.

We tend to spend a lot of time and energy looking for happiness. We look to relationships, money, sex, drugs, power, entertainment, material things, etc. Our mind loves searching for happiness because it's a problem that begs a solution, it seems to make sense to do so and we believe that, once we find it, life will be peachy. Searching for happiness is like your relationship with your back. Your back is awkward to reach, you usually only glimpse parts of it at a time, yet it's always with you and you never doubt it's there. The real difficulty with searching for happiness is that we're looking for something we already have. We are always, already happy! This may seem unbelievable or ridiculous, especially because your mind is probably saying that, based on the past, it can't be true.

We come from a place of unity with God and are born into a world of apparent separation. We usually don't begin to feel separate until some time has gone by. The feeling of separation continues to grow as we develop our identity and see that others have theirs, as well. As the feeling of separation enlarges, our mind starts to do lots of things to try and make up for it: controlling ourselves and others, identifying ourselves as special, solving problems, worrying about the future, seeking enlightenment and so on. Our mind uses the feeling of pain, loss and separation to justify its belief that we are unhappy and then calls many of its dances a search for happiness. The point is that separation is what our mind perceives—not what is. Our filters prevent us from experiencing what is.

It has been proposed that the world is either set up for the best outcome, is random or is designed to fail. Another way of looking at this is that God is either beneficent, doesn't give a damn, or is out to get us. Generally, we believe one or all of these to be true at various times depending on our feelings of the moment. Various models also exist to explain what life is; life is suffering, life is loss, life is what happens while you're making other plans, etc. And, there are many ways of looking at the nature of reality: illusion, conventional reality, multiple planes of consciousness. Asking what is the meaning of life and other questions like that are very different than asking what is the purpose of my life. Asking what is the meaning of life assumes that there is an answer, that you will be able to decide it's the right answer, that you will accept it and, if you're asking another person, that they have it. How do we know what we know? Can we trust what our senses tell us? How much time do we spend looking at what our beliefs are based on? What if life is happiness?

Our minds tend to think in dualities—black or white, right or wrong, good or bad, happy or unhappy; the coin has to be either heads or tails. Our minds prefer this kind of thinking because it's simple and controllable. We think this way because it's the frame that our mind chooses to operate in. Conventional reality says that the flip of a coin is an easy way to make a choice or reach a decision because the coin almost never lands on its edge and if it does, well, you just act like it didn't happen and flip again. But that's only one reality. What about a reality where the coin lands on its edge more frequently? What if you flip the coin over sand or gelatin or in an atmosphere with reduced gravity? Sounds silly but that's our mind saying it's silly. We can imagine as many different realities as we choose, and that can be very helpful to live in this one. Our mind doesn't want to look at different frames of reality because it can't control all the possibilities that come up.

Instead of our mind's black and white thinking we can look at multiple possibilities. Let's use our body as an example. I can feel contracted. I can feel expanded. I can feel both contracted and expanded. I can feel neither contracted nor expanded. I can feel both contracted and expanded and neither contracted nor expanded. That's five options instead of our mind's insistence on choosing only one. In order to control, our mind stops time, usually in the past, and reduces the many possible realities to one frame—the one where it's black or white, heads or tails. Where's the choice? When we feel stuck, it's because we are. We are stuck in the way our mind eliminates choice by seeing only one possibility, while the illusion of choice is maintained. Go to the spa or go shopping or see a movie or read a book or make love or eat ice cream. Yet, what kind of a choice is it when you habitually take that same rigid mind with you wherever you go?

Our mind lives in a reality that is based upon survival and fear. That reality is not particularly helpful to our healing, learning and growth. Our mind prevents us from feeling our unbroken connection with everything and creates the illusion of unhappiness. When we take away our mind's filters, judgments and meanings, we reveal what's always there: connectedness, unity, God. We are always, already happy because unity is our nature. As acceptance grows and we diminish our mind's control and occupy The Mind more fully and more frequently, the continuity of that state and our existence in it becomes self-evident.

* * *

Q: *Some really bad things happened to me as a child. How do I accept them and move on?*

A: We think that the traumas of our past have a death grip on us that prevent us from healing. So what is it, actually, that's holding on? What part of us adamantly refuses to let go? Is it our eyelashes? No. Our left little toe? Unlikely. Our 5th rib? Probably not. Is there any part of our body that really has the capacity to make us believe that what happened 20 years ago is a ghost that will forever haunt us? There seems to be only one part of us that has that ability, our mind. This is not to say that our body doesn't reflect the pain of those experiences. It definitely does. Our body contains, in the skeleton, connective tissue, muscles, organs, etc., echoes of everything that we have not healed. That is why healing work, through the body, provides an excellent side door for sneaking up on our mind. Only our mind has, by its design and function, mechanisms which can convince us that the past is still present. Our mind is largely invisible, yet has more power over us than we can easily grasp. It's a piece of cake for our mind to mix up cause and effect, past and future, thinking and feeling, doing and being, doubt and belief, God and religion, etc.

When we talk about those things from our past that we can't accept, it's very helpful to get clear about what makes them unacceptable. Is it our judgment that the other people involved were wrong because they should have known better? Is it our meaning assignment that we were bad because why else would it have taken place? Is it our misperception of what occurred, that convinces us we're special? Is it our strategy that we can avoid change by refusing to forgive? Maybe some or all of these are true, but looking at each part, individually, allows us to explore what's true for us now, versus the black and white, smushed together picture of the experience that our mind wants to maintain.

It's also helpful to look at what we may gain from not letting go of the past. Are we punishing someone by holding on? Does it allow us to justify our victimhood or martydom? Do we believe that something worse, like a desired yet feared change in our lives, would result from healing that wound? Would friends and family regard us differently if we no longer wore that hurt like a tattoo on our forehead? Would letting go imply that someone might have been forgiven a long time ago? Have the feelings associated with that trauma become so familiar that they are now more like nourishment than discomfort? Again, some or all of these may be true for you. It takes courage and honesty to identify these things because what we may be gaining by holding on appears, on the face of it, to be very little next to the pain that the experience seems to have caused. But despite how whacky our mind looks at times, everything it does is for a very good reason, at least to our mind.

When there are things about our past that we can't accept, then there are also going to be aspects of our current lives that cause us difficulty. We don't get to accept the present while denying the past. Our mind will identify any similarity between what is happening now with what happened before and lump it all into the same category. It's sometimes easier to start with what's not working now and then work your way back to what didn't work then. And, it's often easier to address healing through your body. Since our body's limitations are a direct reflection of what is yet to be healed, we can often circumvent our mind by approaching healing in this way. In doing so, acceptance becomes more like the side effect of healing, rather than the target and because our mind is so good at deflecting any attempt to change what it's holding onto, working through your body is a great way to work around your mind's defenses.

Q: *Without right and wrong and meaning, how do we know who's responsible for correcting problems?*

A: Usually, when we're looking for the responsible party, we actually want to figure out who's to blame. Our mind tells us that as long as someone else has the blame, we're in the clear, we're okay. Blame and responsibility are often confused in this way. "Who's to blame?" and "Who's responsible?" and "Who's guilty?" sound interchangeable and they are, when the intention of the person who's asking is to avoid any ownership of what has occurred. Blame is a strategy used by others to get out of the hot seat. Whereas, responsibility is what we willingly take on when we accept our life and our role in the lives of others.

If we start by wanting to determine whose fault it is, we're already cruising down the right/wrong highway at a pretty good clip with no exits anywhere in sight. If, instead, we start by taking responsibility, the possibilities for a desirable and mutually satisfactory outcome increase significantly. Why take responsibility for something that happened in the next room, the next block, the next town or the next country? Your mind will tell you that it's not your problem, so don't get involved. Interestingly, this is one of those areas that your mind is usually quite happy to not try to control. It seems logical; it's not your life that's been affected, it's someone else's. What could you do, anyway? The problem is too big, too complicated, too far away, someone else's job, etc. When your mind does get active in this area, it's often a way to get involved in the drama, as a spectator, while avoiding the work. Sometimes, depending on the models we had and how much TV we watch, we mistake the drama of the situation for the work of participating in its resolution.

When we look at the world we've created with its art, institutions, wars, religions, technology, science, environmental changes, etc., we like or dislike what we see. We often believe that this is someone else's doing: government, big business, organized religion, God and so on. We usually want to believe that what we see, especially the things we don't like, were not created by us, and therefore, we're not responsible for them. Yet our world is an exact reflection of our humanness. It shows us our successes and failures, our pettiness and fearfulness, our reaching and faltering, our misperceptions and doubts, in effect, a vast tableau of both our mind and The Mind. To maintain control, our mind will want to keep its distance from some or all of this. But the people who create all of this are not an alien race, much as we might like to believe that. They're us! We're them! These are all our creations. Our attempts to separate ourselves from what we don't like are the same mechanisms our mind uses to filter, judge, assign meaning and control. The way we treat friends, loved ones, ourselves and strangers is no different, though on a smaller scale, than what happens all around the planet.

So we also use right and wrong and meaning to distance ourselves from taking on the very responsibility that could change the situation. We draw whatever line suits us in the moment. "I'll just stay away from that uncle because we don't get along." "I'm not going into that office because the boss's secretary has it in for me." "I don't drive through that part of town because it's not safe," etc. There's nothing wrong with any of these, yet, each one causes us to be a little more guarded, contracted, smaller, heavier and cut off.

We are responsible whether we own it or not. Not disowning responsibility allows in the possibility that we can accomplish more than we previously believed. When we accept what is, a new source of courage and strength becomes available and we perceive the world differently. Much of this difference involves no longer seeing events as all negative or all positive. Somehow, the worst disaster creates unforeseen connections and occurrences that offer us new learning and new opportunities. Yes, there is often great loss, yet the loss makes room for unexpected gain.

PART 3

THE PARENTS
OF LIFE PURPOSE

9

SELF-TRUST

Life without a crystal ball

Many of us use words such as hope, faith and trust. We hope that our neighbor recovers from her illness. We have faith in our spiritual leaders. We trust that everything will work out. We use these words because we don't see the big picture. They are a substitute for not having more information about people and events and the relationships between them. These words are about believing in a design and process of life combined with an acknowledgement that all of the details and connections seem beyond our knowing.

When we have sufficient information about the way the universe operates, we gain something well beyond the realm of hope, faith and belief. It's called self-trust. There are several misconceptions about self-trust. One is that you will know what to do in every situation. And, it may appear to others, who lack self-trust, that you do know what to do. Another misconception is that everything is okay with you. After all, if you trust yourself in a variety of situations, then these situations must be okay with you, right? Well, being able to handle things is not the same as liking them. You still have desires and preferences and opinions. What's different is that you tend to be less reactive and more cognizant that things will change. Self-trust gets you unstuck from the child's time line, where it appears that whatever is going on now will last forever. With self-trust, you are aware that you have true power rather than the illusion of control. Self-trust is often confused with self-esteem and self-confidence. Self-esteem is how you feel about yourself, usually in combination with a rating such as high or low. Self-confidence has to do with your ability to perform specific functions like solving math problems, playing basketball or baking cookies. Self-trust, however, is the ability to respond authentically in the moment, without knowing, in advance, what to do and without judgment of the outcome.

Sometimes people are heard to ask, "What should I be feeling?" or they say, "I don't know what to feel about this." This is an example of how our mind controls the feeling process in the absence of self-trust. It's like asking, "What am I supposed to like?" or "How often should I breathe?" Our mind first has to figure out what we're feeling, then it has to assess if those feelings are right or okay or permitted and then, depending on the answer, it does or doesn't allow us to verbalize it. Is there a right way to feel about love or death or pain or God? Well, if you're stuck on right and wrong, there may be and, by looking for the right or wrong answer, you'll only reinforce your mind's control. If, on the other hand, you're feeling whatever is true for you and not judging it, then your mind gets a little smaller and self-trust increases.

Self-trust is closely tied to intuition. We have intuitions all the time but our mind doesn't let them through. Our mind distrusts intuition because it can't control the source. Intuition seems to bubble up from different places in us at different times. This is scary for our mind because it's so unpredictable. And our mind, being the scorekeeper that it is, will continually try to evaluate our intuition in terms of right and wrong as a further attempt to control it. If our mind can convince us that our intuition is unreliable, then it gets to push it away that much more forcefully when it does present itself.

When you listen to people talk, you often hear them use the word, belief. "I believe in God," "I believe in our president," "I don't believe in corporal punishment," etc. We use the word frequently to communicate our position on various things. What we often don't recognize is that when we're talking about our beliefs, we're also talking about our doubts. We rarely say, "I believe I'm 47," "I believe I'm female" or "I believe in gravity." What's the difference? How come there are some things we believe in and some things we have no doubt about?

There is no belief without doubt being present, as well. Our mind bounces back and forth between the two, making it challenging to move on. Doubt and belief are like the two sides of the same coin but they're more subtle than, say, right and wrong. When we use the word, belief, our mind is active. It's looking for a way to sound as convincing as possible while still reserving its right to come back later and say "Well, I'm not wrong because I only said I believed it." Our mind continually hedges its bets and is on the lookout for an escape route, if needed.

Sometimes we talk about a special kind of beliefs called core beliefs. The intention is to elevate some beliefs to a higher level by saying that these beliefs are more deeply held or more intrinsic to our nature. Again, this is our mind's trickery, getting us to think that if we give something a fancy sounding name, it will carry more weight. If belief were actually the core of our being, we'd really be in a mess! Fortunately, we have something much stronger at our core than belief. Our mind, on the other hand, has fear at its core and, with doubt as a major manifestation of that, it can easily make us think that belief is critical to our existence. Belief is still belief, no matter what you call it and as long as it's a belief, doubt will also be present. There's nothing wrong with this, in fact, it's what helps us to move beyond belief. When we catch our mind doing one of its many jigs, by paying attention to the language we use, we're presented with a great opportunity to look closely at what we're doing and that's when the possibility of another choice begins.

With self-trust, you don't need an out or an excuse. With self-trust, a mistake is a mistake, nothing more or less and it doesn't mean anything about you. Equally, when self-trust is present, an accomplishment is an accomplishment, nothing more or less and it doesn't mean anything about you, either. Will you derive more pleasure and satisfaction from your accomplishments and successes than from your mistakes? Probably, because our brain and nervous system are designed to build upon success and pleasure. Yet as self-trust builds, you may find that successes and achievements aren't that much different from mistakes and failures because they are both important parts of something bigger and more essential to our humanness—the process of learning.

When we fully realize that there is no learning without error, like there is no light without darkness, we start to view the whole progression of our lives in a much different way. What changes is that our mind shrinks as we heal. Its agenda stays the same but it's no longer as big and strong and controlling as it used to be. Less mind, more Mind.

* * *

Q: *How do I know when self-trust is present?*

A: There are some important attributes that are closely connected with self-trust: choice, power, freedom and responsibility. They are words we use all the time but how do we know if we have them? Do they exist only as concepts in our minds, or do they manifest in our bodies? How can we increase their presence in our life?

A king is sovereign when he rules autonomously, without the need for external validation. His rule is successful when he wisely employs choice, power, freedom and responsibility for the benefit of his kingdom. These same functions are required for sovereignty in our individual lives. What confines our movement toward new possibilities, new relationships and new adventures is our mind's fear. Our mind fears what it can't control and it also fears the pain of the limitations we have accepted. To change the nature of our existence, in other words, to become an adult, determination is called for. Courage is required to face the truth of our self-imposed restrictions and to let go of our outdated self-perceptions. We demonstrate courage as adults when we honestly face ourselves and others.

Self-trust develops as we have repeated experiences of feeling and recognizing whether we are responding honestly or acting out our mind's denial and pretense. While the input of others can be helpful, most of the time we're on our own so we need to identify an internal measure to know when we are playing out old habit patterns.

Feeling what is true is much easier if I can identify whether, right now, I'm big me or little me. In other words, am I responding from a place that is expanded or contracted? Answering this requires that I can recognize, in my musculature, organs and body, as a whole, the emotional and physical feelings associated with expansion and contraction. When I can feel my contraction, I begin to have choice about altering it.

The ability to recognize who we are, in the moment, and use that information in a helpful way, is directly affected by the judgments we carry about our process. For example, if I recognize, because my stomach or jaw or neck is tight, that the words I just spoke in a conversation with my girlfriend come from little me, that piece of information can be immediately put to use by stopping and changing into big me before saying anything else. However, if the judgment I hold about hearing that contracted part speak is too great, then automatically, the potentially transformative value of the information is lost as my judgments blocks the process of awareness.

Changing little me into big me calls for permission to stop, permission to say that I need a break, an intermission, a moment or a day or a week to get clear about what I'm doing, permission to come back later and continue. Once you've given yourself permission to stop, the rest of the process is a lot easier. You can identify what you're feeling. You can talk with someone you trust who can offer a different perspective. You can do nothing for a while and simply wait for clarity to present itself. You can put yourself in the other person's position and look at things from their point of view. You can pray, meditate, garden, crochet, go fishing; whatever allows you to get out from under the judgment and meaning that you've assigned to the situation. When you do this, however you manage it, you may feel your body become less contracted.

We're so used to the feeling of contraction that it becomes habitual. Our brain loses interest in any signal that is continuous. We sometimes don't even feel the release of muscular contraction because those muscles have been contracted for so long that even though our brain gets the message, we've temporarily lost a way to recognize the associated feeling. Yet, in the same way that self-trust will be absent when muscular contraction exists to any large degree, self-trust will increase as contraction is released. We actually feel bigger and lighter when we are in a state of self-trust.

It's essential to distinguish preference from meaning. It may sound like only a semantic difference to say, "I don't like war," instead of "War is bad," but, to our mind, there's a vast difference. Expressing preference builds self-trust because of the inherent choice, freedom, power and responsibility in statements that begin with "I like..." or "I feel..." or "I want..." Whereas, statements such as, "Liberals are..." and "You should..." and "They can't..." serve, instead, to reinforce the child's world view based on whatever we were taught about right and wrong.

As babies, we had no alternative to having others meet our survival needs. We depended on those external forces and would have died otherwise. We learned for example, that mommies and doctors make our hurts go away. Now, as adults, we still behave as though that were true. But in the same way that no external force can learn for us, neither can it heal us. Others can assist and guide, yet the decision to heal is ours alone. Responsibility exists when we are willing to take over the healing process for ourselves and when we take full ownership of everything that has happened and will occur in our life.

The desirable conditions for learning about self-trust are situations which provide many, many, many (there's a lot of years of conditioning to overcome!) safe experiences and ways to feel, recognize and acknowledge our contractions, chances to witness the judgments, meanings and misperceptions we've created, and possibilities for changing little me into big me. Considering our mind's enormous capacity to deny, pretend, etc., this learning may be most effective with a somatic focus so that recognition of process and change is primarily based on feeling through our body rather than thinking with our mind.

If we could think our way out of fear we would have done so long ago. When we no longer fear being wrong (freedom), we intentionally follow (choice) our desire (power) and are fully accountable (responsibility) for the outcome.

10

CONSCIOUSNESS

The rewards of being a slow learner

So why do we come here? To learn. We are designed to learn. We are an amazing combination of animal skills and learning machine ability. Learn what? Everything. Everything about the physical and non-physical universe. Everything about getting along with ourselves and each other. For what purpose? Evolution. Why bother with all that? Why aren't we just born fully realized and enlightened? Why go through all this pain and fear and learning and healing?

In the same way that we have and are continuing to evolve physically, we are also evolving spiritually. The process will be a lengthy one, though very rapid when considered within the universal timeline. Our ability to eventually occupy, simultaneously, all of the planes of consciousness moves our evolution toward unremitting enlightenment.

Some people think of enlightenment as some spacey, far out, touchy feely, woo woo place, which we can talk about but few, if any, ever reach. It may be more useful to think of it as adaptation. Plants and animals evolve and adapt to better fit their environment. We are adapting toward enlightenment and evolving to fit in the universe. Enlightenment is a process. The more time that we occupy The Mind, the more the process accelerates. It may seem amazing that, in many areas, we have made tremendous technological progress, yet at the same time, we're still killing each other, fighting over ideas and beliefs and religious practices and abortion and laws and food and water and rights and wrongs. How could we have come so far in so many ways and still not be able to get along with each other? How can we use this incredible, huge creative Mind while at the same time being stuck in our tiny, fearful, controlling mind?

In the past several thousand years or so of what we call civilization, where we have some historical records to look at, we seem to be killing ourselves off at a fairly consistent rate. In the past 200 years or so of industrialization and technology, we're still spending a lot of time and energy fighting and dying. When it comes to learning how to be less fearful and more compassionate, it seems to take many lifetimes to grasp and hold onto major life lessons such as acceptance and consciousness. Even within a single lifetime, we appear to need many repeated opportunities to fully integrate what we're learning and to heal. Perhaps we're really slow learners. When it comes to relationships and getting along with each other, it looks like we're still learning the alphabet! While healing can take place in a moment, even in the blink of an eye, we really don't know how much preparation has occurred before a lesson finally takes root. Chances are, the soil has been tilled and fertilized and watered for years before any particular seedling of learning is, at last, able to sprout. While it may appear that healing sometimes occurs spontaneously, we've probably been working on it for quite a while both as individuals and as a species.

What if you wanted to teach a very large number of creatures really challenging lessons like love, responsibility, self-trust, unity, etc? You could say, "This is the way it is, now go live it," and hope that they got it. You could model it or write about it, teach it and train others to teach it, but that would still limit the number you could reach and the information would get altered over time and with transmission. What if you decided that the most effective way was to give these creatures the tools to discover, for themselves, how to evolve and develop consciousness? What if you could create a mechanism, within each of them, that would eventually, through its very workings, reveal these lessons via a process of trial and error. We know that our nervous system is designed so that most of the amazing things we're capable of are based on self-discovery. What if the spiritual and healing lessons we're learning are so challenging for us that it takes many lifetimes to learn them? What if God designed it this way?

Our mind starts out as a survival aid. It helps us make sense of the situation we are born into: the living environment, the people who take care of us, their interactions with each other and ourselves, and their feelings toward us. Lacking the bigger picture, our mind creates stories about how we fit into all of that in a way which supports our continued existence. Potential threats to the process of our development are explained as problems, outside of our mind, which must be solved in order to maintain survival.

Both our brain and our mind have survival as their first priority. Our brain is designed to support our physical well-being and reproduction. It has specific objectives but no need to control the outcome. Our mind, on the other hand, focuses on the avoidance of fear and pain and is completely invested in controlling how all that happens. Using the mechanisms involved in control, our mind is continually revealing to us, by its own processes, how we get in our way, how we slip and slide and fall while denying all that or pretending that we're just standing there minding our own business. In this way, our mind, itself, is the red flag that tells us we're about to step in the smelly stuff. It's our built-in early-warning mechanism.

As we become more conscious and occupy The Mind more fully and more consistently, additional information becomes available. If we choose, we can go back to previous experiences, even those that happened many years ago, and retrieve the desired information. We can recall very early childhood memories that we thought had been forgotten. We can remember things from infancy, being in the womb or even previous lives. The advantages of doing this are several. We get to see that what we have considered as isolated events are really part of a larger pattern and identifying the pattern allows clearer recognition of the choices we have made and the possibility of making new ones. We also come to see that all information is already available in the universe and we have a choice to open ourselves to it. Letting go into The Mind connects us with the universe in a way that makes transparent what our mind continually hides. This is not something we can do through effort or struggle. Like the baby learning to stand, success is based not on trying but on letting go of everything that does not assist the process.

As we come to occupy The Mind more consistently, we begin to realize that there are several kinds of feelings. There's the everyday hostile, righteous, frustrated, tight, resentful, jealous, hurt, cheerful, bored kind of feelings that are the roller coaster of everyday life. These feelings are related to someone or something in our environment and are accompanied by lots of mental stuff. They are learned behaviors and a product of our mind. There's the peaceful, sad, happy kind of feelings that we sometimes experience that seem to come over us or out of us with no apparent relation to anything or anyone. These feelings tend to be experienced more deeply and have no thoughts associated with them. And then, there's the feeling of The Mind, which could be described as being in the flow. It's unlike what we normally experience as thoughts or emotions and is connected to everyone and everything. It is the experience of unity. There are no problems in this state because our mind does not exist there. There's nothing to do, yet you can do whatever you want. This may sound like fairy dust, yet each of us has experienced this, at least once in our lives. Part of why consciousness is such a powerful force for us is that we are continually given tastes of what is possible and The Mind is present, even when we don't recognize it. The Mind is like our best friend who is always ahead of us on our path. Our mind's fear leads us to believe that we're alone, but occasionally we glimpse The Mind as it beckons us to move closer.

The ideas that we don't have choice and that we are not responsible are the basis for our difficulty in moving forward. They keep us stuck in the past and all the pain that contains. We tend to see life as a blessing or a curse depending on the ups and downs of the moment. It is our mind, which labels and categorizes our experiences into bite-size pieces of life so that it can more easily manipulate and control what happens. Yet we have a large body of written information and knowledge which says that there is a realm, variously called source, unity, God or The Mind, that is so far beyond our perceived limitations and everyday experience that our mind continually doubts its very existence.

On an individual basis, change becomes easier and more likely as we develop our capacity to catch our mind in the act of control. As a species, change occurs when enough individuals have shifted into adulthood so that critical mass has been reached and the scales tip in the direction of planetary evolution. In The Mind, time is of no consequence, choice and responsibility are givens and it is readily apparent that unity is our nature. In The Mind, we see that we are always already happy and that life purpose, life lessons and consciousness are all clear and intimately related.

* * *

Q: *Consciousness seems so elusive. I have it for a moment and then it's gone. How do I hold on to it?*

A: It's funny how our mind always gets into the act. As much as we know that life is a continual process of trial and error, learning and change, we still want to hold on to things, as if that would help or be better. Our fear leads us to believe that we're, somehow, not good enough to experience consciousness and our doubt causes us to think it's only a fleeting experience, which may not recur.

Our brain says, "This feels good, let's do it some more" yet has no complaints when more doesn't immediately happen. Our mind, though, wants to seize upon and cling to anything that it interprets as advantageous to its control. How does our mind think consciousness will help it control? It doesn't. But it does want consistency and confuses the need for consistency with any new and attractive change in our lives. So we taste consciousness, we want more of it, and our mind says that the best thing would be to have it all the time! This is another one of those situations where our mind is actually helping lead to its own diminishment, yet, in the meantime, it still gets to control!

Wanting to be conscious all the time is like an infant wanting to walk when it's a week old. Despite the stories you may hear about instantaneous enlightenment, consciousness is an incremental process. The big steps we sometimes take, that seem like a huge leap to a higher level, often feel like they happened in the blink of an eye but we forget about the little steps we've been taking all along.

Consciousness is not elusive because it's hiding or hard to identify. It seems obscure because our mind habitually takes up so much space in our everyday lives, continually clouding what would otherwise be clear. Since consciousness is the new skill that we're developing, trying to make it constant and static, at this point, will actually limit how much of it we have. Like the baby learning to walk, look, instead, at what isn't working and what can be let go of that may be getting in the way.

Consciousness is not only the presence of a connection with people and things around you, it's also the absence of our mind's habitual activity. Our mind's hustle and bustle incessantly shakes things up. When our mind is quiet, the mud settles to the bottom and the clear water becomes visible.

NOTES

NOTES

NOTES

ORDER FORM

On-line – www.LongbowPress.com

Postal orders – Enclose a personal check and mail it, along with this completed form, to

Longbow Press
P.O. Box 4221
Carlsbad CA 92018-4221

Quantity	Cost
1–4	$14 per copy
5–9	$12 per copy
10+	$10 per copy

Prices include shipping and handling.
California residents add $1 per book sales tax.

Name _____

Street Address _____

City, State, Zip Code_____

Number of copies _____ Amount enclosed _____

Area Code & Phone (_____)_____

e-mail _____

Orders are shipped within 2-4 weeks of receipt.

Privacy policy: Personal information is used only for the purpose of processing this order.

ORDER FORM

On-line – www.LongbowPress.com

Postal orders – Enclose a personal check and mail it, along with this completed form, to

Longbow Press
P.O. Box 4221
Carlsbad CA 92018-4221

Quantity	Cost
1–4	$14 per copy
5–9	$12 per copy
10+	$10 per copy

Prices include shipping and handling.
California residents add $1 per book sales tax.

Name _____

Street Address _____

City, State, Zip Code_____

Number of copies _____ Amount enclosed _____

Area Code & Phone (_____)_____

e-mail _____

Orders are shipped within 2-4 weeks of receipt.

Privacy policy: Personal information is used only for the purpose of processing this order.